Praise for *The Most Powerful Brand on Earth*

"Social business is a complex undertaking that can overwhelm even the most seasoned executive. By focusing on people and processes, Chris and Susan get to the core of what social business is: people connecting with people in an organized way."

—Scott Monty, Global Head of Social Media, Ford Motor Company

"We are fortunate to be living through the most important communications revolution in human history. The ramifications of real-time communications—instantly connecting every human on earth with every other human on earth—are even more important than the invention of moveable type and the printing press more than 500 years ago. However, most organizations aren't set up to communicate in the ways that buyers demand. In their book, Chris and Susan share how you can reach people with the valuable information people want to consume and are eager to share—and how that will brand your organization as one worthy of doing business with."

—David Meerman Scott, marketing strategist and bestselling author of *The New Rules of Marketing and PR*

"While creating fans and advocates is the goal for many brands, you can't get there without having engaged employees who understand the value of your fans and how to build relationships with your most passionate customers. *The Most Powerful Brand on Earth* shows you exactly how to do this. Susan and Chris give you the exact blueprint and steps necessary to create a more engaged and socially active employee base. This is critical for cultivating fans and advocates online, and this book shows you exactly how it's done."

—Mack Collier, author of *Think Like a Rock Star: How to Create Social Media and Marketing Strategies That Turn Customers Into Fans*

"Business has changed. And change is hard. This book helps you create an authentically social brand in the wake of huge shifts in business."

—Ann Handley, coauthor of *Content Rules: How to Create Killer Blogs, Podcasts, Videos, Ebooks, Webinars (and More) That Engage Customers and Ignite Your Business*

"Social business and enterprise social networks now play a key role in changing how we work, where we work, when we work, and even why we work. Chris and Susan's book shows how these trends change the workforce and chronicles the impact to brands. This step-by-step guide tells you how to take your organization to the next level."

—R. "Ray" Wang, Principal Analyst and CEO, Constellation Research, Inc.

"Fundamental to moving from 'doing social' to 'being social' for a brand is recognizing that people are the channel. Susan and Chris clearly put their deep, real-world experience to work and articulate how to empower the people behind the brand—your employees and partners—on social media. This book covers the why, what, and how with clear examples and actionable next steps. Must read!"

—Ragy Thomas, CEO of Sprinklr

"Today's true leaders are not just the ones who create the best products, but also the ones who breed new generations of leaders, unleash the power of their employees, and empower organic advocacy. In the social era, advocacy is where the influence is. Pick up this book and learn how to become the most powerful brand on earth."

—Ekaterina Walter, cofounder and CMO of BRANDERATI, *Wall Street Journal* bestselling author of *Think Like Zuck: The Five Business Secrets of Facebook's Improbably Brilliant CEO Mark Zuckerberg*

"Social media are not just a collection of digital marketing tactics. They are the way a growing percentage of clients and prospects find the information they need to solve their business problems. Connecting your best experts to the clients and prospects with whom you want to develop a relationship is not optional. You either do it well or get left behind by competitors who do it better than you. If you really want to learn how to do it well, read this book."

—James Mathewson, author of *Audience, Relevance, and Search: Targeting Web Audiences with Relevant Content* and the forthcoming *Outside-In Marketing: Using Big Data to Drive Content Marketing*

"*The Most Powerful Brand on Earth* offers communicators, marketers, and executives a thoughtful and complete understanding of the implications for their companies when it comes to activating and enabling a social workforce."

—Ethan McCarty, Director, Enterprise Social Strategy and Programs, IBM

"I've had the pleasure of working with both Susan and Chris for years, and have always considered them two of the real leaders in social media—read this book to find out why. Every company wants to unlock the formula of unleashing their employees and customers in social media on behalf of its brand. Unless you've figured it out yourself, you need this book."

—Mike Moran, author of *Do It Wrong Quickly*

"Brand influence has reached a nexus of Darwinian change, and *The Most Powerful Brand on Earth* is the guide for the evolved to succeed and thrive as a new species in the global business ecosystem, thanks to Ms. Emerick and Mr. Boudreaux."

—Rawn Shah, author of *Social Networking for Business*; Forbes.com blogger: Connected Business column

The Most Powerful
Brand on Earth

The Most Powerful Brand on Earth

How to Transform Teams, Empower Employees,
Integrate Partners, and Mobilize Customers to
Beat the Competition in Digital and Social Media

CHRIS BOUDREAUX
AND
SUSAN F. EMERICK

PRENTICE
HALL

Upper Saddle River, NJ • Boston • Indianapolis • San Francisco
New York • Toronto • Montreal • London • Munich • Paris • Madrid
Capetown • Sydney • Tokyo • Singapore • Mexico City

The publisher offers excellent discounts on this book when ordered in quantity for bulk purchases or special sales, which may include electronic versions and/or custom covers and content particular to your business, training goals, marketing focus, and branding interests. For more information, please contact:

> U.S. Corporate and Government Sales
> (800) 382-3419
> corpsales@pearsontechgroup.com

For sales outside the United States, please contact:

> International Sales
> international@pearsoned.com

Visit us on the Web: informit.com/ph

Library of Congress Control Number: 2013945063

ISBN-13: 978-0-13-311539-0
ISBN-10:   0-13-311539-9
Text printed in the United States on recycled paper at R. R. Donnelley in Crawfordsville, Indiana.
First printing: August 2013

Executive Editor
Bernard Goodwin

Senior Development Editor
Chris Zahn

Managing Editor
John Fuller

Project Editor
Caroline Senay

Copy Editor
Stephanie Geels

Indexer
Ted Laux

Proofreader
Kelli Brooks

Editorial Assistant
Michelle Housley

Cover Designer
Chuti Prasertsith

Compositor
Shepherd, Inc.

From Susan: To my loving husband, Mark, who has stood by me through all of life's opportunities and challenges with unwavering support. And to my beautiful daughters, Mary and Grace, may you come to realize that with passion, dedication, and hard work anything is possible—always stay true to yourself and follow your dreams.

From Chris: To the most important people in my life: Zachary and Caroline.

CONTENTS

PREFACE

Brands that empower employees and customers generate significantly greater awareness and revenues while also decreasing the cost of marketing, selling, and customer service. However, employees must engage in public, real-time conversations. And most people are not professional communicators.

Enabling employees and partners in modern business requires new skills, business processes, governance, measurement, and infrastructure. In addition, leaders must learn new ways of managing risk while helping employees build and manage external relationships in real time. Nearly every industry is affected, and this book provides frameworks, guidelines, and case studies for people to navigate the change for their organization.

How This Book Is Organized

Chapter 1, Web of Trust: The Case for the Social Work Force, explains why a brand should consider empowering employees and partners in social media. We provide data from a wide range of sources to explain how (1) permanent changes in human communication are making online advocacy a critical priority; (2) people trust people, now more than ever; and (3) your brand's official communicators cannot do it alone.

Chapter 2, Help Your People Do Well, explains how to help your people create relationships and engagement that create business value. Specifically, we show how to plan the roles and skills you will need, then, how to attract, onboard, support, and measure the people whom you empower in social media.

Chapter 3, Influence: It's Complicated, explains (1) how the nature of online influence is often misunderstood; (2) how influence works online; and (3) reasonable expectations for how a brand can create and leverage online influence.

Chapter 4, The Power to Sway: Helping Employees Build Advocacy Online, provides a proven framework to plan, execute, manage, and measure the development and optimization of relationships with online influencers through employees and partners.

Chapter 5, You Will Measure New Things in New Ways, gives you a framework for measuring (1) business outcomes; (2) the performance of your people; and (3) the performance of your social empowerment program.

Chapter 6, Safety and Security, describes the security, privacy, and regulatory issues that brands must resolve to ensure that employees, the brand, and other stakeholders are safe and secure when employees and partners engage in social media on behalf of the brand.

Chapter 7, How to Begin, explains how to get the support you will need from leaders, program participants, and other stakeholders in your organization. The chapter includes (1) how to build a business case for this kind of program; (2) how to align your program to the goals of the executives who will fund or support you; (3) how to use pilots to prove the concept and build support; and (4) how to use early adopters.

Chapter 8, Build Your Team, details the team that you will need in order to run a program that delivers business value through employees and partners in social media.

Chapter 9, Manage the Journey, explains the role of culture in this kind of program and how you can structure your strategy and your program to succeed within your organization's culture. Culture and change management will make or break your program, so the chapter also provides a proven framework for managing the change journey that your organization and your people will undergo.

Finally, **Chapter 10, The Future of the Social Work Force,** examines emerging or slowly evolving trends that will affect social empowerment programs five to ten years in the future.

ACKNOWLEDGMENTS

Alone we can do so little; together we can do so much. —Helen Keller

There were so many people who have been a part of our journey through the years that we would like to recognize for their teamwork, collaboration, support, and guidance. Without them this book would not be possible.

To the IBM Management Team, especially Maria Arbusto, David Bruce, David Chamak, Ben Edwards, Jon Iwata, and Ethan McCarty for their open leadership. To the IBM Social Insights practice leaders, especially Bill Chamberlin and Amy Laine, who've led the enterprise to understand the value of social intelligence and analytics. Cheers to the "Dynamic Trio"! To the extended group of IBM colleagues who worked to advance our strategy through many years, especially Cleveland Bonner, Catherine Brohaugh, Colleen Burns, Laura Cappelletti, Christian Carlsson, Adam Christensen, Phil Corbett, Stacy Darling, David Davidian, Joyce Davis, Anna Dreyzin, Jennifer Dubow, George Faulkner, Willie Favero, Jeanette Fuccella, Randy Gelfand, Steve Gessner, Nigel Griffiths, Linda Grigoleit, Keith Kaplan, Katie Keating, Scott Laningham, Dawn May, Maurice Mongeon, Katherine Motzer, Jeanne Murray, Jennifer Okimoto, Pauline Ores, Younghee Overly, Martin Packer, Tony Pearson, Kasper Risbjerg, Joshua Scribner, Mark Schurtman, Rawn Shah, Elisabeth Stahl, Luis Suarez, Paul Turnbull, Delaney Turner, Jennifer Turner, Todd Watson, Steve Will, Tina Williams, Tiffany Winman, and Kevin Winterfield.

To our friends and colleagues who passionately and willingly shared their perspectives or influenced our work over the years, in alphabetical order: Sinan Aral, Constantin Basturea, Neil Beam, Will Bottinick, Liz Bullock, Warren Butler, Tom Chernaik, Craig Daitch, Adam Edwards, Greg Gerik, Sam Fiorella, Paul Gillin, Paul Greenberg, Chad Hermann, Tom Hoglund, Bill Howell, Joe Hughes, Rob Key, Mark Kovscek, Alex Laurs, Lindsey Loughman, Robin McCarthy, Scott Monty, Mike Moran, Jeremiah Owyang, Bryan Pedersen, Ric Rushton, David Meerman Scott, Jasper Snyder, Gene Spafford, Philip Stauffer, Sabrina Stoffregen, Jeff Thibodeau, Jeffery Treem, Ted Ulle, Danna Vetter, Ray Wang, Allen Webber, Dean Westervelt, and Steve Wick.

ABOUT THE AUTHORS

Chris Boudreaux helps large brands transform their business operations for ROI through social and digital media. He also led development of social media offerings and served as a solution architect for social media solutions at a global management and technology consultancy. In past years, he led online product and market strategy efforts at multiple global technology brands.

Chris began blogging for business in 2005. In 2008, he developed his first Facebook app and created SocialMediaGovernance.com to help organizations get the most from their social media efforts. In 2011, he coauthored *The Social Media Management Handbook* (Wiley & Sons), and his studies of social media have been referenced by corporations, governments, industry analysts, and nonprofit organizations around the world.

He also led business development and marketing at two online start-ups, including a digital advertising start-up acquired by Glam Media.

Prior to his career in digital and social media, Chris was an officer in the U.S. Navy, where he flew helicopters and led the anti-submarine warfare division aboard USS Yorktown.

Chris holds an M.B.A. and an M.S. in computer science from the University of Chicago, a master of aeronautical science from Embry-Riddle Aeronautical University, and a B.S. in management from Tulane University.

Susan F. Emerick leads global enterprise social business programs for IBM, a company with more than 430,000 employees. A passionate marketer, adjunct professor, and speaker, Susan enjoys navigating the redefinition of marketing "as we know it" driven by emerging technology and big data. She consults with marketers globally about applying social and digital media to foster long-term, high-value relationships with clients, prospects, partners, colleagues, and communities.

Beginning in 2008, Susan helped to establish the social insights practice at IBM to continuously apply social listening insights to marketing planning and social engagement strategies. As a result, IBM was awarded the 2010 SAMMY award for Best Socialized Business.

In 2011, Susan was named to the elite iMedia Top 25 Internet Marketing Leaders and Innovators, an annual list of cutting-edge creative professionals, strategists, and technology innovators. As an active member of the Word of Mouth Marketing Association Research and Measurement Council, Susan uses her expertise and creative curiosity to influence the standards and principles of word-of-mouth research and measurement.

Connecting with the Authors

Chris Boudreaux

Blog:	http://socialmediagovernance.com/blog
LinkedIn:	http://linkedin.com/in/chrisboudreaux
Twitter:	@cboudreaux
Email:	chris@socialmediagovernance.com
Phone:	(415) 692-1250
Web Site:	http://socialmediagovernance.com

Susan Emerick

Blog:	http://susanemerick.com
LinkedIn:	http://linkedin.com/in/sfemerick
Twitter:	@sfemerick
Email:	emericksf@gmail.com
Phone:	(248) 552-5797

Web of Trust: The Case for the Social Work Force

"Before a revolution, everyone says it's impossible. Afterward, everyone says it was inevitable."

— Anonymous

Permanent changes in human communication are making trust-building and online advocacy critical priorities for brands. Trust in traditional media is declining while trust in social media is increasing. In addition, people trust information and official corporate channels less, while trusting employees more. The ways that brands connect with customers must change.

Social media are all about people and relationships—not brands, not technology. People.

While most of us understand that online advocacy drives sales, many people do not realize that *sales correlate strongly with the number of **people** who advocate for a brand, not the number of **online posts** or **messages** advocating for a brand.*

This is a critical point to understand: if you measure social media performance in terms of posts or messages or conversations, your decisions are potentially off track. If you really want to use social media effectively, you need to think in terms of *people.* Ultimately, social media should help your brand develop relationships with people.

And the most important strategy question that we must ask ourselves is, "How will our brand effectively and efficiently nurture relationships with people in social media?"

After all, relationships require effort. They aren't always predictable. And they typically require at least two parties to give and take together.

In many cases, it is far more natural for your customers and other audiences to develop relationships with your employees and your business partners rather than with brand-owned teams or channels. Why? Here are a few reasons.

First, we all tend to form relationships with people we perceive to be like ourselves. When you expose the diversity of your employees to your audiences, you dramatically increase the chance that your audience will find and establish a relationship with someone they perceive to be like themselves.

Second, each of your employees has a certain expertise. Different people understand different parts of your products, for example. People trust experts, and they want to hear from those experts when they have a question or a need for information.

Third, a brand is not a person. Brands do not empathize. They do not feel passion. But people do.

Ultimately, brands that empower their employees in social media give a tremendous gift to their audiences in the form of expertise, diversity, and passion.

But empowering employees and partners in social media is not simple. You have to do more than write a policy, publish training, and give people permission to engage. In reality, including more people requires a different approach.

For example, when you add a large number of employees to your social media engagement, you can easily overwhelm your audience with repetitious content, producing a negative experience.

As another example, we have found that traditional PR approaches to influence outreach simply do not work when you start adding lots of employees and partners to the process. The tools are inadequate, and it takes new processes and skills to coordinate development of external relationships across a large number of employees.

If you want to empower employees to build advocacy for your brand, you'll need to provide a support structure—just as you would with any other organizational capability. In addition, large-scale empowerment in social media usually requires critical change management and cultural support, especially when your employees already have a full-time job. After all, most of your employees are not professional communicators.

And this is not just about your employees. Different industries use different roles to communicate with the market. Some brands use channel partners or suppliers. Insurers use agents in local neighborhoods or contact centers; technology companies use channel partners and sales people; pharmaceutical brands use sales people and researchers; and so on.

In the past few years, some people have suggested that brands should hire journalists to create compelling content on behalf of the brand. And we believe that many brands could bolster their marketing and communications organizations in that way.

However, that approach only goes so far and, in fact, simply will not scale to the levels needed by brands today. Specifically, it is far easier to train experts to publish than it is to train journalists to be experts. As stated by Shel Holtz, Principal at Holtz Communication + Technology, "It's important to understand that SMEs-as-brand-journalists is *part* of the future. Great writers will always have value and companies will always be able to use them. But the idea of hiring writers to write about areas of expertise that are alien to them makes a lot less sense than teaching people who are *already* experts how to write well."[1]

Too many social media "strategies" today focus on tools that will be implemented; impressions, friends, or followers; or campaign goals they will

---

1. Holtz, Shel. "Subject Matter Experts Will Play a Big Part in the Future of Brand Journalism." 23 October 2012. http://bit.ly/Holtz-Experts.

achieve. Too few social media strategies specify the relationships they intend to nurture and the business value that the organization expects to accrue from those relationships. We hope this book gives you the tools to change that within your organization.

In the remainder of this book, we explain how you can create a systematic program that empowers your employees and business partners to leverage their professional expertise and skills to build a web of trust that supports and protects your brand.

We show you how to select, train, and retain them. We also show you how to navigate the complicated world of influence and how to protect employees and your brand from online threats to privacy and security. We explain how you can build a program team that suits the scale of your organization—be it large or small—and how to evaluate the readiness of your organization as well as measure the contribution of employees engaged in social media. And we show you how to bring executives on board so you can get the funding and resources that you need to succeed.

Finally, we discuss emerging trends that will make the social employee a basic fact of life and a requirement to compete for almost all brands.

If you believe nothing else, believe this: online advocacy drives sales. And the most cost-efficient way to create sustainable online advocacy is to empower your employees. The remainder of this chapter explains why.

The Source of Brand Power Today

Online advocacy drives business. When advocacy increases, sales increase (with a 30- to 60-day lag). When advocacy decreases, sales also decrease. In fact, 53 percent of changes in sales can be attributed to changes in the number of people advocating for a brand online.[2]

The same holds true for any action that you want people to take, whether it's buying, voting, or applying for a job: when more people online endorse an action, more people are likely to take the action—online and offline.

---

2. Northwestern University and MotiveQuest. "Remarkable Implications: The Correlation between Online Advocacy and Offline Sales." Chicago, IL: Northwestern University, November 2011.

People Need to Hear a Message More Times to Believe It

But advocacy isn't easy to create. In fact, people are growing more skeptical in general and harder to convince of anything.

As of 2012, 63 percent of people need to hear something three to five times to believe it.[3] In 2011, it was 59 percent, so it increased by 4 points between 2011 and 2012. Simply stated, people require more repetition to believe any new message that they hear.

As Figure 1.1 shows, 72 percent of people need to hear something three or more times to believe it.

The trend holds true around the world. For example, in Japan, 82 percent of people need to hear something 3 or 4 times to believe it. So repetition

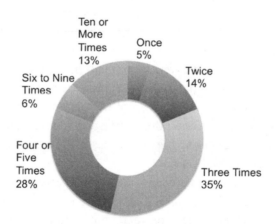

How many times in general do you need to hear something about a specific company to believe that information is likely to be true?

Ten or More Times 13%

Once 5%

Six to Nine Times 6%

Twice 14%

Four or Five Times 28%

Three Times 35%

Survey Population: Informed Publics ages 25 – 64 in 25 countries

Figure 1.1 *People need to hear information about your company three to five times to believe*

Source: Edelman. "2012 Edelman Trust Barometer." http://bit.ly/Edelman-2012.

---

3. Edelman. "2012 Edelman Trust Barometer." http://bit.ly/Edelman-2012.

is key; if you want people to believe something, you probably need to tell them 3 to 5 times. Maybe more.

Traditional Media Are Losing Share to Social Media

At the same, time, the McKinsey Global Institute reports that radio and television lost their shares of American media consumption, while social media gained significantly.[4] In fact, more than one billion people spend an average of seven hours per week on Facebook alone.[5]

In addition, business decision makers, just like consumers, increasingly turn to social and professional networks as a primary source of news, information, ratings, and reviews of products and services.

In addition to spending more time engaged in social media, people are also trusting more in social media. While traditional media sources such as news are still the most trusted, trust in social media increased by 75 percent. Trust in other online sources, made up of search engines and news/RSS feeds, increased by 18 percent from 2011 to 2012 (see Figure 1.2).

Nielsen found similar results in its 2011 Global Trust in Advertising report[6], which surveyed more than 28,000 Internet respondents in 56 countries (see Figure 1.3). In that survey, 92 percent of consumers around the world said they trust media such as recommendations from friends and family above all other forms of advertising—an increase of 18 percent since 2007.

According to the Nielsen survey, online consumer reviews are the second most trusted source of brand information and messaging, with 70 percent of global consumers indicating they trust messages in online reviews, an increase of 15 percent in 4 years.

In a survey of 1,500 Dutch consumers, nearly two-thirds (65 percent) said they find information posted on social media to be reliable, and 40 percent said that they find posts made on social media to be trustworthy. In addition, frequent social media users believe that financial posts on social media are just as reliable as information published in traditional online media, such as news sites and newspaper Web sites.[7]

---

4. "Wordy Goods." *The Economist online.* 22 August 2012. http://bit.ly/WordyGoods.

5. Gartner, Inc. "Gartner Forecast: Social Media Revenue, Worldwide, 2011–2018." Stamford, CT: Gartner, Inc., 25 June 2012.

6. Nielsen. "Global Trust in Advertising and Brand Messages." 10 April 2012. http://bit.ly/NielsenGlobalTrust.

7. "Impact of Social Media 2012." ING Bank, Social Embassy and InSites Consulting. 2012.

How much do you trust each of the following places as a source of information about a company?

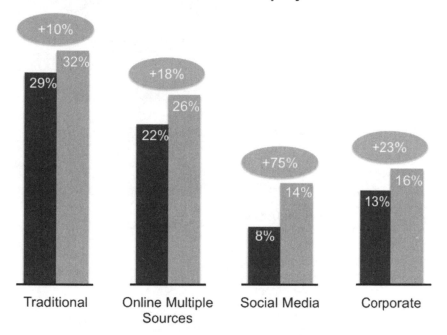

"Trust a Great Deal"; Informed Publics ages 25 – 64 in 20 countries.

Figure 1.2 *People now trusting multiple media*
Source: Nielsen Global Trust in Advertising Survey, Q3 2011.

Although nearly half of consumers around the world say they trust television, magazine, and newspaper ads, confidence in each of those media declined significantly between 2009 and 2011. In fact, confidence in television fell by 24 percent, confidence in magazine ads fell by 20 percent, and confidence in newspaper ads fell by 25 percent in just 2 years. According to the advertising agency Edelman, in France and Germany, trust in television news and newspapers fell by ten or more points. China saw double-digit decreases in television as a trusted source, plunging from 74 to 43 percent. Newspapers in that country didn't fare well either (down by 20 points to 34 percent).

But trust in social media jumped: microblogging sites and social-networking sites went from virtual distrust at just 1 percent each to being

To what extent do you trust the following forms of advertising?

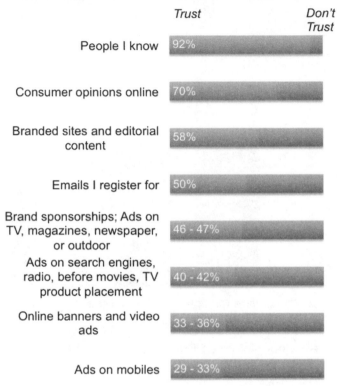

Trust   *Don't Trust*

People I know	92%
Consumer opinions online	70%
Branded sites and editorial content	58%
Emails I register for	50%
Brand sponsorships; Ads on TV, magazines, newspaper, or outdoor	46 - 47%
Ads on search engines, radio, before movies, TV product placement	40 - 42%
Online banners and video ads	33 - 36%
Ads on mobiles	29 - 33%

Figure 1.3 *Trust in different forms of advertising*
Source: Nielsen Global Trust in Advertising Survey, Q3 2011.

greatly trusted by 25 percent and 21 percent, respectively—a likely reflection of the rapid growth in social media usage within China.

As Liz Bullock, Director of Social Media & Community at Dell, describes, "After seven years of work in the field, we have concluded that social media impacts every aspect of the customer experience and life cycle in positive ways, and in some respects, impacts the customer life cycle more than any other medium."[8]

Even our traditional source of news—journalists—relies on social media to get their information. In surveying more than 613 journalists in 16

---

8. Bullock, Liz. Personal interview. April 2013.

countries across North America, Asia and the Pacific, and Europe in April and May 2012[9], Oriella PR Network discovered that more than half of journalists (55 percent) use social channels such as Twitter and Facebook to find stories from known sources, and 43 percent verified stories using these tools. Further, 26 percent of respondents said that they used social media to find stories from sources they did not know, and almost one in five (19 percent) verified work in progress from sources unknown to them. The figures are even higher in the United Kingdom, with 75 percent of journalists using social media to research news from known sources.

Scott Kirsner, innovation columnist at *The Boston Globe* and author of *Fans, Friends and Followers: Building an Audience and a Creative Career in the Digital Age,* says, "I listen better to people directly involved than people paid to pitch. In-person connections are where it's at. I want to see companies in their natural habitat: when they innovate, not when they have a PR agency."[10]

Social Media Impact Search Engine Results

And if you care about your company's placement in search engines such as Google, Bing, or Yahoo!, you need to understand that social media have a growing impact on where you land.

In 2010, Matt Cutts of Google gave the first official statement that Google uses links in Twitter and Facebook as a signal in placing search results.[11] At the time, no one was sure how social media really impacted search engine results.

On June 7, 2012, SearchMetrics published analyses of search results from Google for 10,000 popular keywords and 300,000 Web sites to determine the attributes that correlate[12] with a high Google ranking.[13] The chart in Figure 1.4 shows the attributes that most correlate with high ranking in Google search results.

---

9. Oriella PR Network. "The Influence Game: How News Is Sourced and Managed Today. Oriella PR Network Global Digital Journalism Study 2012." June 2012. http://bit.ly/InfluenceGame.
10. Scott, David Meerman. "Get Famous Fast: Helping Entrepreneurs Win at Media Relations." WebInkNow.com. 19 November 2012. http://bit.ly/Kirsner.
11. Google Webmaster Help. "Does Google use data from social sites in ranking?" 17 December 2010. http://bit.ly/GooMaster. Video.
12. Correlation in this case means Spearman's rank correlation coefficient, defined at: http://bit.ly/SpearmanCo.
13. SearchMetrics. "Facebook and Twitter Shares Closely Linked with High Google Search Rankings." 7 June 2012. www.searchmetrics.com.

Most Influential Factors
Spearman Correlation: 0.25 – 0.37

- Facebook Shares
- Backlinks
- Facebook Total
- Facebook Comments
- Facebook Likes
- Tweets

Second-Most Influential Factors
Spearman Correlation: 0.10 – 0.15

- % backlinks rel = nofollow
- Keyword in Domain Name
- % Backlinks With Keyword

Third-Most Influential Factors
Spearman Correlation: 0.03 – 0.05

- % Backlinks With Stopword
- Image Count
- Keyword in URL
- Keyword in Description

Figure 1.4 *Social media impact search engine results*
Source: SearchMetrics. "Facebook and Twitter Shares Closely Linked with High Google Search Rankings". 7 June 2012. www.searchmetrics.com.

At the time of this study, social media created five of the top six factors that correlate with search engine rank.

So, if you want people to take a certain action, you need to create advocacy; and to convince people of something new, you likely need to give them the message three to five times. And you will need to use social media to do it.

In the past ten years, the world in which advertisers crafted brand messages to capture the imagination of a mass market and then broadcast those messages via one-way channels disappeared.

But that is not all. Oh, no. That is not all.[14]

---

14. Seuss, Dr. *The Cat in the Hat*. Boston: Houghton Mifflin, 1957.

Respondents who replied "extremely credible" or "very credible" to the following question:

If you heard information about a company from one of these people, how credible would that information be?

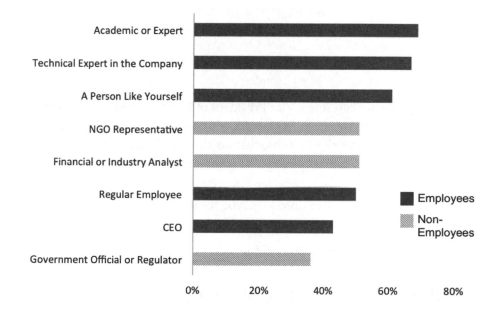

Figure 1.5 *Credibility of sources for information about a brand*
Source: Edelman. "2012 Edelman Trust Barometer." http://bit.ly/Edelman-2012.

People Trust Employees More than Official Brand Sources

Although trust determines where people buy, people don't trust brands or CEOs as much as they used to. Instead, people trust employees. In fact, people trust any type of employee more than the CEO. See the chart in Figure 1.5 from the 2012 Edelman Trust Barometer.

In one example of how this can really impact a business, IBM found that online traffic generated by IBM experts in social media converted seven times more frequently than traffic generated by other IBM sources.[15]

---

15. Emerick, Susan. "IBM Select Social Eminence Program, 3Q 2012 Measurement Framework Pilot." Detroit, MI: IBM, September 2012.

As stated by Scott Monty of Ford Motor Company:

> We know that word of mouth is the most powerful method of marketing, as raw and uncontrolled as it is. We also know that having advocates who can represent the brand through their own passion points is crucial. What better advocates does a company have than its own employees, who are usually engaged in word-of-mouth marketing, whether or not they realize it? Harnessing that enthusiasm and knowledge, and specifically encouraging and empowering employees to apply what they've always done to social media, has to be the foundation of any company's efforts if they want to survive.[16]

In the words of Scott Roen, Vice President of OPEN Forum and new product development at American Express, "Businesses may not have supreme power, but they can work with those that do, the individual influencer."[17]

So, if you want to convince people of something, you need to do the following.

• Tell them three to five times—maybe more.

• Use social media.

• Let your employees do the talking.

Your Brand's Official Communicators Cannot Do It Alone

In our experience, roughly ninety percent of the posts within most online conversations mention no brand. Instead, most of the posts discuss the category and the motivations that drive people within the category.[18]

For example, in online conversations about saving for college, more than 90 percent of the conversation mentions no brand whatsoever. Also, in the online conversation about diets, more than 90 percent of the conversation mentions no brand names. In any conversation, you can typically expect that less than 10 percent of the conversation will mention any brand name.

---

16. Monty, Scott. Personal interview. February 2013.
17. Dubois, Lou. "Why Social Influence Matters to Business." 31 March 2011. Inc.com.
18. Northwestern University and MotiveQuest. "Remarkable Implications: The Correlation Between Online Advocacy and Offline Sales." November 2011.

Can your dedicated marketing and communications staff keep up with all of that? Probably not, for two reasons: (1) you can't produce enough content, and (2) in social media, people—not brands—are the channel.

You Can't Produce Enough Content

In 2012, author and marketing consultant Mark Schaefer[19] wrote:

> Here is the sneaky little secret of content marketing. You don't need to have the best product or service to win. You don't need to be the best marketer to win. You don't even have to create the best content to win. You just need to be first and overwhelming.[20]

But most brands struggle to keep up. According to the Content Marketing Institute (CMI) and MarketingProfs, 29 percent of North American marketers surveyed said their biggest content marketing challenge is producing enough content.[21] That challenge—up from 20 percent of respondents in 2011—supplanted concern over content quality, which took a big drop from 41 percent of respondents in 2011 to 18 percent in 2012. Overall, the report showed that almost two-thirds of B2B content marketers find it difficult to produce enough content, while about half are still struggling with producing the kind of content that engages.

In Social Media, People Are the Channel

Your employees have connections that your brand does not. Think about the total connections your brand has on all the social networks where you have brand-owned accounts. How many connections does your brand have? Now, think about all of your employees who are active in social media. How many connections do your employees have? And who has more in total: your brand, or your employees?

---

19. Mark Schaefer was named a Power 50 social media influencer by *Forbes Magazine*, a Power 150 marketing blogger by *Advertising Age* magazine, published two books on social media, one of which earned the Book of the Year award from B2B magazine.
20. Schaefer, Mark. "The Ultimate Content Marketing Challenge." 6 November 2012. http://bit.ly/ContChallenge.
21. Pulizzi, Bob, and Handley, Ann. "B2B Content Marketing: 2013 Benchmarks, Budgets, and Trends—North America. Marketing Profs and Content Marketing Institute, 2013. http://bit.ly/B2BBench.

For nearly every brand, the employees have far more connections online. They always will. Why? Because, in social media, people are the channel, not brands.

Dion Hinchcliffe of Dachis Group said it best in our interview, declaring, "In social media, companies don't have much social capital. People do."[22]

The IBM example on page 11 demonstrates that content in social media is far more effective when it flows through real people—not brand-owned, officially logo'ed, social accounts.

But you can't just blast your corporate messages through your employees' social media and expect your audience to engage. In fact, it takes much more than compelling creative, and clever messaging to get your audiences to advocate for you; it's about relationships, not transactions.

Further, a brand is not a person, and a brand-owned social media account is not the same as a personal social media account. If your content is to be effective, then, when it passes through your employees, it will change in at least the following three ways.

- First, your people will modify the content to fit what they know about their audience, which will be slightly different than what you know about the larger audience that you target.

- Second, they will modify the content's language or form to make it unique, such that the audience is not overwhelmed by repetition.

- Finally, your people will modify the content to fit their personal style and how they engage their audience.

To understand why, let's explore the evolution of music.

Your Content Must Change to Fit the People Who Channel It

David Byrne of Talking Heads published a book in 2012 in which he explains that music evolves to fill the space where it is performed.[23] In general,

---

22. Hinchcliffe, Dion. Personal interview. November 2012.
23. "Byrne, David: How Architecture Helped Music Evolve." February 2010. http://bit.ly/12rRaj6. Video.

writers and performers evolve the style of their music to fit the venues where they usually perform. For example, Byrne explained that the music he wrote that sounded great in the nightclub CBGB didn't sound quite right when he performed it in Carnegie Hall. In CBGB, the audience yelled, danced, and fell down, and there was very little reverberation in the room. Therefore, the music that sounded best at CBGB was loud, with clear rhythms. When venues like Carnegie Hall came into prominence, audiences were expected to be very quiet, and the room created significant reverberation. Therefore, the music was able to support extreme dynamics; quiet parts could be heard; and the music did not need to be as rhythmic.

Have you noticed that we often refer to different online social properties as venues? And have you noticed that different types of content tend to prevail in each social venue?

In general, the kind of content that works best in these different venues is very different than the kinds of content that worked well in traditional online venues. In social media, the venue makes the content evolve into something that works well within that venue. Just like music evolved to fit each new venue, for as long as music has existed.

Gregorian chants would not be successful in CBGB, and marketer-written, copy-pasted tweets will not work when simply passed through employee social media accounts.

As David Meerman Scott explained in his WebInkNow blog:

[S]uccess using the different forms of online content is evolutionary to the way the content is consumed. The best content evolves to fill the new media (such as blogs, YouTube videos, Tweets, photo sharing, and the like). Each new way to create content means a new form of content is best suited for the media.[24]

Of course, the critical difference between social venues and traditional online venues is the fact that people are inherent in the venue. Actually, people *are* the venue.

---

24. Scott, David Meerman. "How Content Works." 26 September 2012. http://bit.ly/ContentWorks.

1 Permanent changes in human communication make online advocacy a critical priority

- More than one billion people spend an average seven hours per month in Facebook alone[1]
- 63% of people need to hear something 3-4 times to believe it, an increase of 4 points from 2011 to 2012.[2]
- Costs of digital production are so low that any employee can establish a global audience, on their own
- 53% of changes in sales can be attributed to changes in the number of people advocating for a brand online.[3]
- Customers and potential customers can advocate for a brand at every stage of the purchase funnel.

2 Online advocacy drives sales.

- Trust determines where people buy.
- People trust people, now more than ever.
- Trust in social media grew 75% between 2011 and 2012.[2]
- When hearing information about a company, the most trusted sources from within the company are (1) a technical expert in the company and (2) 'a person like yourself'[2]
- Social media make it easier for all of us to access opinions of people like us, thereby increasing our reliance on people like us

3 Your brand's official communicators cannot do it alone

- One-third of all marketers and two-thirds of B2B marketers feel challenged to produce enough content
- 90 percent of online conversations are not about brands at all—they are about categories and the motivations that drive people within those categories[4]
- In conversations about any brand, the brand typically creates less than 10% of the conversation
- Employees have connections that the brand does not
- Employees who are recognized as thought leaders can decrease the costs of engaging external audiences
- Brands already have the most difficult asset to develop: enthusiastic and knowledgeable employees

[1] Source: Gartner Forecast: Social Media Revenue, Worldwide, 2011 – 2018. Gartner. June 25, 2012.
[2] Source: 2012 Edelman Trust Barometer. http://www.edelman.com/trust.
[3] Source: Remarkable Implications: The Correlation Between Online Advocacy and Offline Sales.
[4] Source: "Beyond the Dashboard: Remarkable Implications. The Correlation Between Online Advocacy and Offline Sales". MotiveQuest. November 2011.

Figure 1.6 *Summary of reasons why brands should empower employees in social media*

Your Next Steps

1. Understand the extent to which your brand is trusted relative to other brands in your industry.
2. Determine the potential impacts on your brand if your competitors empower their employees and partners in social media.
3. Determine the areas of your business that might benefit from more socially empowered employees.
4. Identify programs in which your brand plans to invest, which could benefit from socially empowered employees; understand the results they plan to achieve, and how socially empowered employees could help to advance the programs' goals.
5. Determine the extent to which you use social media to develop relationships with audiences, versus simply broadcasting brand messages in social media.
6. Determine the extent to which journalists engage your brand as a source of news about your industry, not just news about your brand.
7. Determine the extent to which you are deliberately using social media to improve your brand performance in organic search results.
8. Determine how much value your brand could achieve by migrating investments from traditional paid media into socially empowered employees.

2

Help Your People
Do Well

"This isn't Margaritaville. You can lose the parrot head, my friend."

— Susan Emerick

Many brands have given their employees permission to use social media, published a social media policy, and offered training on the use of social venues. But that level of support leaves a lot of potential value on the table. This chapter explains the kinds of support that a brand should provide to fully empower employees and partners in social media.

Why You Must Help Your People

Many brands avoid empowering their employees in social media because they do not want to dis-intermediate the marketing team from customers, or they do not want employees creating brand assets that the brand does not own. Some brands fear that employees in social media could damage brand reputation or violate regulations and create liability for the brand. Some brands just do not know how to begin.

"My team hears from other groups every day, looking for advice about where to begin," says Ethan McCarty, IBM's director of social strategy and programs. "The most common questions start with 'are we allowed to', or, 'can you point us to a good example'—which led to our choice to post our social computing guidelines publicly and regularly publish stories about social media successes on our intranet and our external websites."[1]

Regardless of how a brand feels about its employees in social media, nearly every brand today has employees who are active in social media and employees who talk about their brand in social media.

Those employees engage in social media for a wide range of reasons. In many cases, employees get into social media because their partners and customers demand it.

As one example, 3M structured employee empowerment at the corporate level in response to clear demand from their partners and customers. Greg Gerik, who is a global social media leader at 3M, says, ". . . [O]ur partners and customers look for 3M employees to be socially engaged. Before we had formal processes and training, our teams naturally found a way on their own."[2]

While almost every brand today can find employees using social media to discuss their products, services, working conditions, and so on, the brands that achieve the most value deploy corporate resources to empower their employees in social media.

Simply asking employees to parrot brand-generated messages through their personal social media may help the brand to gain small amounts of reach or engagement, but it is not a sustainable strategy for engaging audiences and developing relationships online. It is easy to do, so a lot of brands do it; however, that approach fails to respect the relationships between

---

1. McCarty, Ethan. Personal interview. March 2013.
2. Gerik, Greg. Personal interview, November 2012.

employees and their audiences, so it does nothing to help employees create a differentiated and effective presence online.

Specifically, when people simply repeat brand-generated messages, they lose the ability to attract *people like me*[3], thereby diminishing their ability to build trust and advocacy online. (See Chapter 1, Web of Trust: The Case for the Social Work Force, for more details.)

As stated by Jon Iwata, Senior Vice President of Marketing and Communications at IBM, "Some forward-thinking companies . . . are providing the training, tools and encouragement to make their employees expert at using social media. In doing so they are creating a competitive advantage."[4]

In general, the greatest potential value of socially empowered employees can be achieved only when the brand aligns employee activities in social media with brand goals. And you should do so across the organization. As stated by Danna Vetter, Vice President of Consumer Marketing Strategy at ARAMARK:

> Each of our businesses that are active on social has different strategies to meet their business needs. So the metrics we use to determine success vary by strategy. We expect employees to set goals and objectives to meet their business' needs, just like they would in any marketing campaign. Our job is to give them the opportunity to be successful and provide them the tools that allow them to be.[5]

Brands that build the competitive advantages of socially engaged employees quickly encounter a host of internal and external challenges, including potential conflict between brand goals and the employees' personal goals for their own professional reputations. Often, those two sets of goals may not align completely, and it takes some effort for the brand to keep it all working together.

In 2012, Alexandra Samuel of *The Wall Street Journal* referred to socially engaged employees who build a personal reputation as "co-branded" and observed that:

> Co-branded employees may exist largely below the radar now, but that's changing fast, and employers need to start preparing for the ever-greater challenges they pose for managers, co-workers and companies. Their

---

3. The phrase "people like me" refers to findings by advertising agency Edelman that people tend to place the most trust in others who are perceived to be like them. Source: Edelman. "2012 Edelman Trust Barometer. http://bit.ly/Edelman-2012.

4. Iwata, Jon. IBM Social Jam. 10 February 2011.

5. Vetter, Danna. Personal interview, November 2012.

activities can either complement a company's own brand image or clash with it. Companies that fail to make room for co-branded employees—or worse yet, embrace them without thinking through the implications—risk alienating or losing their best employees, or confusing or even burning their corporate brand.[6]

Ultimately, brands need to respect the employee's desire to develop their own reputation—or the reputation that the employee may already have—because the greatest impact occurs when both the brand and the employee understand and integrate each other's strategies and plans.

Some of the questions that a brand must resolve include the following.

- How do we manage potential differences between each employee's personal brand and the organization's brand?
- How should managers balance responsibilities among socially engaged employees and those who are not—for example, bloggers and non-bloggers within a team?
- How do we protect confidential, proprietary, and customer information? (We address this question in more detail in Chapter 6, Safety and Security.)
- To what extent should we support or encourage social publishing during work hours?
- Can or should we make social engagement mandatory for some roles?
- How do we ensure that people who contribute to content receive proper credit?
- What is a social media presence worth, and how should we reward or compensate employees who achieve the goals that we define?
- If an employee creates a new digital asset that portrays the brand, who owns that digital asset?
- How should our policies change to protect the brand and employees?

---

6. Samuel, Alexandra. "Your Employee Is an Online Celebrity. Now What Do You Do?" *Wall Street Journal Online.* 29 October 2012.

Figure 2.1 summarizes some of the impacts on work force management, also often called *human capital management,* which an organization should anticipate when empowering employees in social media.

In order to ensure that you properly align a social employee empowerment program with brand goals, you should engage the business units and functional teams whose employees you will empower and whose business goals you will support. You will achieve value for your organization to the

Work Force Management Areas	Example Considerations
Human Capital Planning	• Engage all teams involved to define program goals • Involve people with the power to take action
Skill Development and Assessments	• Add new skill requirements, job role definitions and assessment criteria • Connect personal goals to real work goals and processes
Training and Education	• Help employees understand the business value • Create and distribute training and education • Develop new leadership and management attitudes and behaviors • Incorporate real-time and public aspects in training • Provide risk and crisis management guidance • Enable formal and informal coaching and mentoring
Rewards and Retention	• Determine the value of social employees to the brand • Estimate effort to retain employees with influence or advocacy • Create rewards to encourage knowledge sharing and management behaviors • Design rewards that improve performance and motivate action to promote advocacy
Knowledge Management	• Unlock employee knowledge and insights • Listen and respond to employee recommendations and issues • Measure success according to increases in employee productivity and capacity; degree of authority and influence

Figure 2.1 *Considerations for human resource management when empowering employees in social media*

extent that you connect employee empowerment with real work goals, business processes, and outcomes that the business wants to achieve.

"For our team, this means using social media to make our departmental goals and our managers' annual goals explicit to the whole company," said Ethan McCarty, IBM's Director of Social Strategy and Programs. "For example, we post sample goals in our on-line community for our team to customize. And the managers on our team publicly post their *personal business commitments* to create transparency and clarity across the department."[1]

Especially engage the people in those teams who have the power to help you take action regarding the goals of your social employee empowerment program. Chapter 8, Build Your Team, provides ways that you can engage leaders across your organization to build support and engagement in your program.

Social media require your people to engage in real-time conversations, online, and often in public view. But most of your people are not professional communicators. So they will need new skills, and you will need to help them develop those skills while taking into account considerations described in Figure 2.1.

Scaling this kind of program will require that you embed social media skills into the employee development and evaluation processes of your organization. Eventually, you will need to add social skills to your organizational skills taxonomy; in most organizations, this helps to define roles throughout the organization.

Some employees' job responsibilities will change, and the Human Resources organization will need to update job role definitions and skill requirements. These new skills will dictate employee performance evaluation criteria that may be new to the brand. You might find it helpful to define different skill levels at different career levels, and thereafter, skill development plans and assessments should change to support the new job role definitions, requirements, and career advancement.

During training and education, begin by helping your people to understand the business value that can be created when employees and partners build trust and advocacy online. To help them truly understand how the real-time and public aspects of social media engagement work, provide real-life examples that illustrate the types of behaviors you want them to demonstrate.

In particular, tell employees what they *should* do in social media, instead of what they *should not* do. Demonstrate this "what to do" approach across various roles in your organization, such as sales, marketing, and product specialists. Describe the benefits that the brand expects to achieve in terms of quantifiable business outcomes. Doing so will make the training more meaningful to employees.

TRAINING EMPLOYEES: IBM CENTER FOR ADVANCED LEARNING[7]

To help train employees in social media, the IBM Center for Advanced Learning uses a progression of simulations they call "Show me. Guide me. Let me." The system includes modular courses that can be combined to train employees from beginning to advanced levels.

When they began to develop the content for the courses, the center first delivered the training through a series of Web conferences. Each Web conference was recorded and then published in the internal intranet for employees to consume at their leisure.

Now, the training includes three progressive stages of simulations that gradually help learners develop the skills they need to engage in social media on behalf of IBM. Those stages are:

1. **Show Me (Demonstration):** Video simulations demonstrate the steps of procedures to learners, while also showing text that describes the process. Audio is often also provided to explain the steps to learners.
2. **Guide Me (Guided Practice):** Learners participate in the simulation by clicking the tools they would use in real life, but the tools are simulated. Throughout the simulation, text or audio guides learners through the process within a safe environment where learners can make mistakes without interfering with actual customer information in a live system.
3. **Let Me (Assessment):** Learners click through a series of steps within a lab exercise to achieve desired results, but no guidance is provided during the exercise. Learners rely on their knowledge attained in steps 1 and 2 to complete the simulation. This is the most effective way to know whether learners understand the process.

Given the quickly evolving nature of social and digital media, you will need the ability to quickly create and distribute training or education to

---

7. Emerick, Susan F. Personal interviews. November 2012 through March 2013.

your people—especially as new channels, best practices, or policies emerge or fade. To see how Microsoft empowers product experts to rapidly produce, distribute, and continually update product content and training, see the case study entitled Real-time Product Training at Microsoft. This approach could easily be used to train employees who are active in social media and also to keep them continually equipped with the latest information about your brand.

REAL-TIME PRODUCT TRAINING AT MICROSOFT

In the old days, when Microsoft launched a new product, they would tell their sales people to stop selling for a week, travel to headquarters in Redmond, and consume a week of training. Studies showed that sales people did not sufficiently retain the training as well as Microsoft would like. Further, when the training was delivered, the products were not finalized, so the information delivered to learners always changed before the product released to market, and even thereafter.

For one product launch, Microsoft decided to take a new approach. Instead of creating a week of professionally crafted training content, flying sales people to Redmond, and running a week of classroom training, Microsoft decided to use social media including podcasts and a network of experts to create short, consumable content that let sales people get the information they needed, when they needed it, and always with the latest product information included.

First, Microsoft staffed two internal evangelists who visited internal product experts, gave them a Web camera and a microphone, and showed them how to create internal podcasts. The experts were then encouraged to create content about their products in multiple formats, including video, audio, and PowerPoint slides. Finally, Microsoft created an internal Web site for sales employees and channel partners to easily find the content created by the experts.

Sales people could go to the internal site and search for a product or for a particular question from a client. They could find answers and the content they needed because Microsoft had already determined who the experts were and given them the tools to create the content as needed.

Employees and partners could download slides created personally by the experts, which they could then use with their own clients.

Sales and channel staff were able to get just the content they needed, exactly when they needed it, and it was always the latest information, even as the product changed over time.

Profiles of each expert were displayed alongside the content they created, along with presence information indicating when the experts were available or online. Employees could then contact the expert for questions and conduct a phone call or Web conference with the expert, if needed.

Visitors to the site could rate effectiveness of the content, and they could also rate the experts as providers of content. The ratings helped people to quickly find the most effective content.

As a result, employees absorbed the information more consistently and retained it to a greater extent.

In addition, Microsoft saved significant travel and content production costs, with 500 podcasts published per month. Further, the content had a much longer effective life because the experts could continually update the content as needed. Microsoft estimated that they would have needed to spend $30 million to achieve the same outcomes through traditional training approaches. And all of this was accomplished while keeping sales people in the field, with customers.

We think this approach can make a lot of sense for brands that want to enable their employees to talk about their products—especially in dynamic industries where products or competitors change rapidly.

Of course, none of this will succeed if your company leadership and management do not support employees engaging in social media. So, you will need to determine the leadership and management attitudes and behaviors necessary to support social employee empowerment. Then, you must embed the desired attitudes and behaviors into the relevant leadership development programs in your organization.

As part of defining the value to your employees, you will first need to understand the value that social employees create for the brand. Then, determine the level of effort that you are willing to expend in attracting and retaining such employees. The answers may vary across teams within your organization.

With those answers determined, you can begin to think about the rewards and recognition that you can provide for the various behaviors that you will encourage among your social employees.

Throughout the process of onboarding, supporting, and occasionally bidding farewell to people who participate in your social empowerment program, you should think about the ways that you will unlock, preserve, and expose the depth and breadth of employee knowledge and insights that should be shared throughout your teams.

Finally, ensure a reliable and consistent process for listening to and responding to employee recommendations and issues. Measure success according to increases in employee productivity and capacity to achieve business goals and to foster brand advocacy, not simply the amount of effort employees put in. Then, determine thoughtful and efficient ways to reward employees for participating in knowledge management activities.

How to Help Your Social Employees

In our experience, the activities required to properly empower people in social media can be organized into seven areas of activity, as follows: [8]

1. Plan
2. Attract
3. Onboard
4. Support
5. Transition
6. Optimize
7. Lead

Figure 2.2 summarizes the above activities, and the remainder of this section explains each component.

Plan

Successful employee empowerment begins with a plan. In this stage, you will complete three types of activities, as follows:

1. Business alignment
2. Team design
3. Role design

Each of these is described in the following sections.

---

8. "Your social employees" can include people who are employees of your brand, contractors, channel partners, and more.

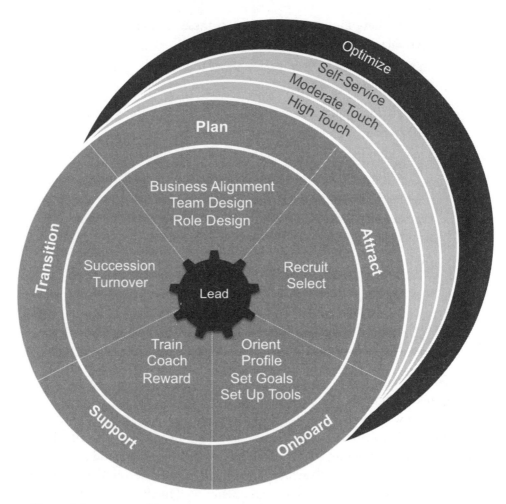

Figure 2.2 *Social employee empowerment lifecycle*

Business Alignment

In order to understand the current state of your employees in social media, ask the following questions:

- Which business topics will your employees discuss online?
- To what extent do your employees discuss topics related to your brand in social media?

- Do they have the expertise to discuss these topics in a knowledgeable manner?
- In which venues do they discuss those topics?
- Where do they participate most actively?
- Which target audiences engage in those conversations with employees?
- Do employees represent your brand, or only themselves, when discussing the topics that matter to your brand?
- To what extent do employees publish versus listen?
- Do they have a degree of authority among the people in their online community?
- To what extent do your competitors' employees possess authority in the same online communities?
- How would you like the above factors to change?
- How much would it be worth to your brand to change the factors above?

Answering the above questions and creating an inventory of engaged employees helps you to understand what you need to do.

As you work to determine the organizational goals that your program will support, collaborate with the leaders of the business units or functional teams that the program supports. And help them to understand how your program can help them to achieve their goals. Then determine the order in which you will take the steps to implement social media empowerment for people in their organizations.

Specifically, you will not be able to deploy this program to the entire organization at once. Instead, prioritize internal teams for enablement, and manage expectations with their leaders. Ensure that everyone understands when you will be able to support their goals and empower their people in social media.

Team Design

Once you understand the organizational goals that you need to support, you can think about how you will organize your teams to achieve those goals. For example:

1. Will you empower one person per subject area, or multiple people per subject area?
2. Will you empower people in one location, or across global regions?
3. How much time commitment can you expect from each participant? This will depend largely on the extent to which their management supports their participation.
4. To what extent will your organization's marketing, PR, and brand staff participate in the program? Will they provide support, tools, or content to the people you empower?

Role Design

During this step, you will define the roles and domains of expertise that you wish to activate in social media. Your selection criteria should be based on your program requirements and the business outcomes you plan to support.

Employees must be segmented to determine which training, support, and tools they require and receive. Employee segmentation also determines the policies, rights, and privileges that apply to each employee. Some job roles may not be appropriate to activate or may require restrictions on their social media activity. For example, employees with access to the private data of your customers may need different tools than people with no such sensitive access. See Chapter 6 for more information about protecting the safety and security of employees, customers, and your organization.

Determine which roles in your organization are able to support brand outreach based on goals of your program and the extent to which each employee is expected or allowed to participate. Then, prioritize the segments of your employees and define the order in which you will empower each role type. For example, you might choose to empower product managers first, then product development staff, and market researchers last.

Finally, based on the information above, define the roles that socially empowered employees can play within your program. Specify how a role will be different when supporting marketing goals versus supporting recruiting goals. Perhaps they will use different tools, they may need different skills or experience, and they might set different goals for professional development.

Example: IBM

Figure 2.3 summarizes the resource allocation structure that IBM created for its global program that enabled employees in social media at three primary levels of support.

In this IBM example, we see that IBM divided employees into three broad segments, as follows:

1. Thought leaders and subject matter experts who receive the highest levels of support through a program named *IBM Select*. These employees receive personal coaching and support throughout their participation in the program. They receive a monthly scorecard on their performance in social media, and they also collaborate actively with marketers and a social strategist. The social strategist coordinates social media strategies and tactics for a go-to-market program. Chapter 8 provides more information about the social strategist role.

2. Software architects and specialists receive a less intensive level of support, in a program named *Forward Thinkers*. These people are supported by a set of custom tools, including an expertise locator, which helps people find others in the company based upon their expertise. They receive community-based coaching and support through online tools that let people connect and share experiences. Their activities and results are measured to provide feedback that improves their performance in social media. These employees also interact with the social strategist to ensure that their online presence and social media activities align with business goals.

3. All employees can access online support through an internal portal named *Digital IBMer Hub*. They can access self-service metrics, content, and training. They direct their own development

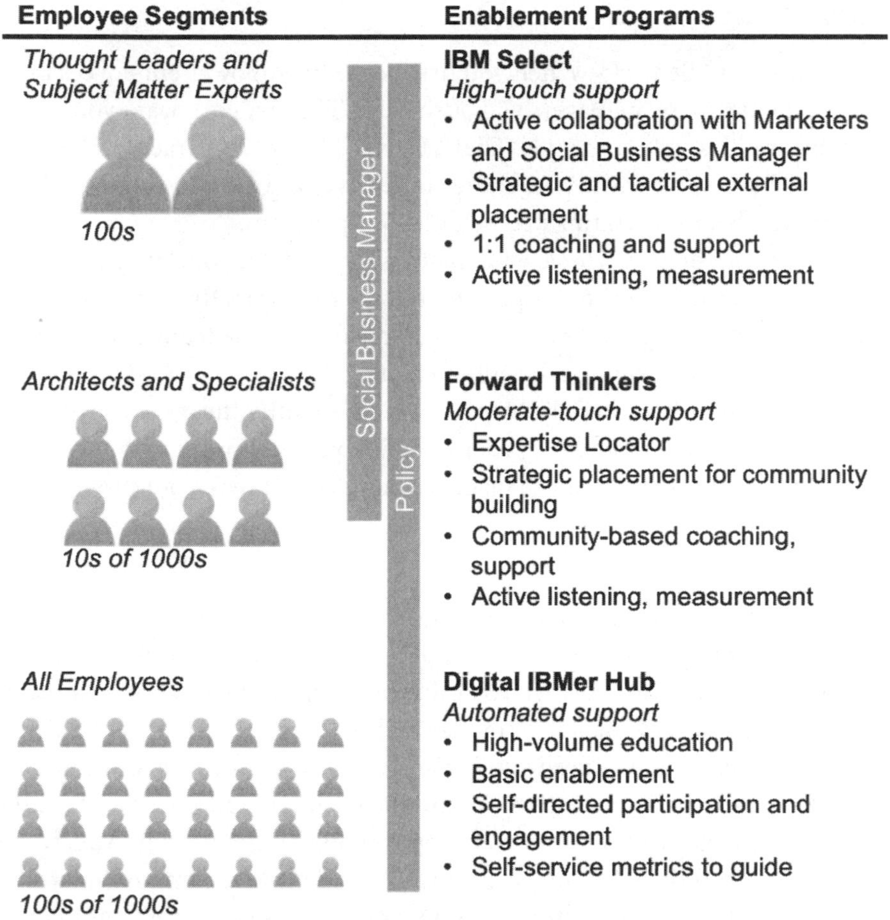

Employee Segments	Enablement Programs

*Thought Leaders and
Subject Matter Experts*

100s

IBM Select
High-touch support
- Active collaboration with Marketers and Social Business Manager
- Strategic and tactical external placement
- 1:1 coaching and support
- Active listening, measurement

Architects and Specialists

10s of 1000s

Forward Thinkers
Moderate-touch support
- Expertise Locator
- Strategic placement for community building
- Community-based coaching, support
- Active listening, measurement

All Employees

100s of 1000s

Digital IBMer Hub
Automated support
- High-volume education
- Basic enablement
- Self-directed participation and engagement
- Self-service metrics to guide

Social Business Manager

Policy

Figure 2.3 *Tiered enablement and support model for social employees at IBM*
Source: Emerick, Susan F. Personal interviews. November 2012 through March 2013.

of social media skills. Guidance is available through online tools that help employees to align their social media activities with brand goals, to the extent employees choose to do so.

Attract

The Attract stage includes the following two activities:

1. Recruit
2. Select

Recruit

Recruiting can be tricky. When you first begin to empower employees in
social media, many managers will push back. They will not want you adding
responsibilities to their people. They will not want you distracting their people. You have to be sensitive to those concerns and prepare to address them
before you begin recruiting people into your program.

When you identify people who might participate in your program, determine whether you should speak with their managers first. Or maybe you
should speak with a senior executive responsible for the team, get that person's support, and then speak with the manager.

Think about this carefully. Map out a plan. Identify the persons with
whom you will speak and the order in which you will speak with them.
Communications with your managers can make or break your program.

Select

The most important requirement in the candidates you recruit will be deep
knowledge and passion around the topics, products, or services that your
program will support. Further, you must prioritize individuals who already
possess a measurable degree of market influence in the communities that
matter to your brand—ideally online and off. The most successful employees
will have the expertise, the passion, and the desire to build trust and credibility with their network in ways that support your program goals. And, when
we say "communities," we mean groups of people with a common interest,
regardless of which Web sites or online tools they use to share their interest.

Also, consider these criteria in your selection process for those employees
who will receive personal support.

- Employees should be comfortable in collaborating, commenting,
  and publishing in social environments.
- They should feel comfortable with and find personal value in
  creating relationships through digital media.
- They must demonstrate a commitment to sustained activity in
  social media where they continually evolve their skills and participation to achieve personal and business objectives.
- They should be willing to participate in brand-owned research
  and social media listening activities that analyze their social
  graph, with the goal of enhancing their professional network.

You can ask each employee the following questions in an initial selection stage.

- Are you present in social media?
- If so, where?
- To what extent do you publish?
- Where do you participate most actively?
- Do you have a degree of authority among the people in your online community?

Getting answers to the questions above and creating an inventory of employees who are engaged online helps you to understand the level of effort that you must invest to support business goals through your employees. A number of tools are available to help you inventory employees who are active in social media. Their capabilities range from letting you manually enter social media accounts of your employees, to allowing employees to enter their own accounts via OAuth[9], to tools that use natural language processing to identify posts that indicate the person is an employee of the brand.

Onboard

The Onboard stage includes the following activities:

1. Orient
2. Profile
3. Set goals
4. Set up tools

Orient

In orientation, you should educate employees on the value of building trust and credibility online. Help them to understand how their personal engagement can benefit them personally, as well as benefitting the brand. When they first join the program, many employees will not understand the level of effort and commitment that is required to develop an effective online presence. They also will not understand the potential value for them personally. Help them to understand how it can benefit their careers and how it can

---

9. OAuth is an online authorization standard that lets people authorize third-party access to their social media account without sharing their account credentials (login).

create value for the brand. This is a tremendous opportunity for the employees, but they may not see it right away. It is your job to explain, just as you must do with stakeholders across your organization.

A typical orientation agenda begins with an overview of the program, including benefits of participation, expectations and time commitment, training resources provided, program milestones, and desired outcomes.

Orientation should also include an assessment of the employee and development of a profile that will guide their engagement in social media, as well as their professional development in social media. Figure 2.4 shows a sample employee assessment.

Profile

You will need to establish a system to track the people in your program. Such a system should allow individuals to describe their expertise, their social footprint, and other meaningful characteristics, such as skills they want to develop. As each person's knowledge and skills evolve, they should update their profile so that other participants can always find people with similar interests and developmental goals.

The profile system should also provide a method for assessing employee skills, proficiency, and preferences. That is the only way to properly align their goals and the support you give them to ensure their success in the program. As cited by Gallup Leadership research:

> [W]hen . . . leadership fails to focus on individuals' strengths, the odds of an employee being engaged are a dismal 1 in 11, or 9%. But, when . . . leadership focuses on the strengths of its employees, the odds soar to almost 3 in 4, or 73%. When leaders focus on and invest in their employees' strengths, the odds of each person being engaged goes up **eightfold**.[10]

Consider approaching the assessment and personalized planning through the following steps:

1. Inventory each participant's social footprint to understand the social venues they use and how they use them.
2. Understand each person's motivation for getting involved and remaining engaged in social media.

---

10. Rath, Tom, and Barry Conchie. *Strengths Based Leadership: Great Leaders, Teams, and Why People Follow.* New York: Gallup Press, 2009.

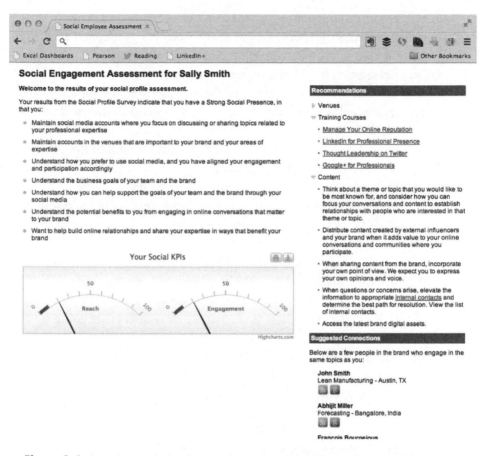

Figure 2.4 *Sample personalized report from an automated assessment tool for social employees*

3. Assess the employee's preferred online behaviors to determine the employee's comfort level with various methods of engaging online. For example, do they only read what other people publish? Do they comment on other people's content? Or do they create content on their own?

4. Determine the most effective ways to mobilize each employee according to their strengths and preferences. Also determine how you will empower them to utilize their skills, preferences, and strengths.

5. Create an action plan or roadmap for the individual that aligns their current skills, personal goals, and business goals. Such an action plan or road map might include the following:

   a. Recommended education and training.

   b. Communities, user groups, or forums that are relevant to the individual's expertise and the business objectives they will support.

   c. Digital content the employee might incorporate into the content they produce or promote.

   d. Insights about relevant influencers, and guidance on how the employee should interact with them. This could include goals for developing relationships with the influencers and the employee's network.

   e. Performance measurement: what you will measure, how you will measure it, and how the employee can use those measurements to improve their effectiveness.

   f. Speculation about how performance assessments are going to impact each individual's professional standing.

   g. Safety and security guidelines, such as policies for social media, information security, etc.

   h. Clear agreements about the ownership of social media accounts and data.

   i. Any other relevant guidelines or policies.

   j. Deadlines for each action or step in the plan.

Greg Gerik of 3M believes, "It is key that each person understand their personal influence. Show them how they can impact the ecosystem; where they are starting, and where they can go."[2]

Figure 2.5 shows how employees tend to evolve their skills in social media for professional purposes, and Figure 2.4 shows a sample employee assessment, delivered through a Web-based assessment tool. The purpose of profiling employees who are new to the program is to understand where they are on this path, to determine the appropriate level that they should try to achieve, and then to define the actions required to help them evolve accordingly.

The remainder of this chapter explains how you do that.

Figure 2.5 *Typical evolution of a social employee*

Set Goals

Ultimately, you should set each employee's goals so that they support the goals of the business. When you work with an employee to determine their goals, you should begin by discussing the business goals that you intend for them to support, and the audience(s) that they will engage to support those goals. Figure 2.6 shows an excerpt of a document that one organization used to define personal goals for a social employee.

After you clarify the target audience and business goal to support, you should then help the employee understand any relevant research that will guide their social media engagement. In this case, based on the goal of customer retention, we see that this employee will need to engage in only a few online forums where customers tend to seek help with a product they purchased.

Target Public	Current Customers
Business Goal	Customer retention: increase product upgrades and transactions per customer
Research Findings	Product conversations occur in a few online forums,· and primarily involve customers seeking help with products after purchase
Business Opportunity	Engage with existing customers in forums to: • Explain the latest product features • Address concerns of people who are considering upgrading • Acknowledge and share customer testimonials
Personal Goals	• Earn 10 reputation points in a high-priority customer community by the end of Q3 • Achieve the Advisor level in a high-priority customer community
Tactics	• Suggest new uses to existing customers • Subscribe to community blogs and comment on posts where you have relevant expertise • Subscribe to content posted by identified influencers • Subscribe to topics that are relevant to your expertise • Create assets that illustrate the benefits of upgrading

Figure 2.6 *Example goals for a social employee*

In this example, the opportunity for the business is to help customers in the target segment to understand the latest product features and to address concerns of customers who are considering upgrading their product. In addition, the business would like to acknowledge customer testimonials, to encourage supportive customers, and share testimonials to spread information that might be helpful to other customers. Ultimately, the business expects these activities to create advocacy for the brand.

In order to help support the goals of the business, the employee can achieve measurable goals (shown in Figure 2.6) within those online communities, where customers discuss the brand's products. In this case, the employee will take actions that increase their reputation within the online community.

Finally, Figure 2.6 specifies tactics that the employee can execute to achieve their personal goals and, ultimately, to support the goals of the business.

Set Up Tools

Many employees who join your program will need help selecting and configuring their tools. Most social employee programs require employees to use the following kinds of tools:

- **Monitoring and Engagement:** Tools that let employees monitor online conversations and exchange messages with their audiences. Examples include HootSuite, Radian6, Sysomos, Brandwatch, tracx, RSS readers, and many, many more.

- **Collaboration Platform:** As you empower more employees in social media, you will need a platform for knowledge management and internal collaboration. Examples of such tools are provided in the section below entitled "Train."

- **Performance Scorecard:** You will almost certainly provide a scorecard of metrics to some of your employees to help them understand their progress and key performance indicators, and you will need to ensure that they are able to access and interpret their scorecards. Some organizations provide scorecards in Excel, and some use Web-based tools that integrate metrics from multiple sources.

- **Content Management:** Your organization or your program may use a content management system that is separate from your collaboration platform. For example, marketers may store digital content in such a content management system for marketing campaigns.

Support

Every employee will achieve greater success with the right support from your organization. The key is to determine the right balance of empowerment and accountability for each employee or each employee segment.

The Support stage includes the following activities:

1. Train
2. Coach
3. Reward

Train

Your employees have worked long and hard to cultivate their professional expertise. And staying relevant in the age of social networking requires that they frequently and proficiently use online channels to connect, share knowledge, and collaborate with peers, prospects, and clients. In order to do so with success, most employees benefit from some degree of training. They may need new skills, or they may need to learn new tools. Your program will achieve more success as you provide the right training, at the right time, to each employee in your program.

In some cases, you may need to overcome assumptions that your employees hold about their existing skills and knowledge of social media. Greg Gerik[2] at 3M says, "There is wide misunderstanding of social networks and programs. Many people make the assumption that, 'I know what this is because I do it in my personal life,' but their personal experience and knowledge doesn't translate to business."[2]

Most social media leaders with whom we speak share his experience. As a result, you will need to develop a curriculum that supports your employees. Some employees may be natural writers and content creators, but the majority probably are not, and they will need training and coaching.

Of course, training should also help employees understand how to mitigate the risks of social media engagement, and we discuss those activities in Chapter 6.

In addition, social media tools evolve continually, and your training program will be challenged to keep pace with those changes.

To help employees learn specific social media tools, we suggest three approaches:

- **Training Vendor:** If you don't have the skills and expertise to develop a training and enablement program internally, you'll need to establish an agreement with an external training provider. Whichever route you choose, you'll need to ensure that the core program is agile and stays abreast of the latest emerging technologies, tools, and their changes. Then, let your employees consume training, as desired, from that provider.

- **Software Vendors:** Regularly survey employees for tools and venues that interest them most and align to brand goals, and buy or host training from those vendor(s). The simple reality is that your employees will need to use different tools across your organization. We have seen organizations attempt to pick one standard tool for engagement in social media, and those standardization efforts always fail. They fail for a number of reasons. First, different tools are better for different purposes. People who sell usually need a different engagement tool than people who work in Public Relations, for example. Second, when you empower employees in social media, many of your employees will already have tools that they prefer to use, and it will not make sense to force them onto a new tool—especially when they may be using free tools. Third, your employees who are early adopters of new technologies will constantly experiment with new tools, and you want to nurture that experimentation, then spread their expertise to other employees. As a result, you will have lots of employees using lots of different tools, and you will need to pick only a few vendors where you use company funds to purchase training.

- **Internal Collaboration:** In your internal collaboration platform, give employees a place and a process for sharing best practices and lessons about their engagement tools.

Social employees at IBM use IBM Connections for internal collaboration. Within that tool, they host multiple communities. One such community, named the Digital Community of Practice, is used by the Marketing and Communications team to share best practices. In addition, each social strategist (described in Chapter 8) hosts and manages their own internal community for the social employees they support.[7] The social strategist uses it as a centralized hub for sharing and disseminating information, such as brand messaging, analyses of external influencers, and research that helps social employees improve their effectiveness and efficiency. Such a collaboration platform provides extensive knowledge sharing, improves productivity, and allows you to unlock the depth and breadth of employee knowledge and insights by listening and responding to employee recommendations and issues.

According to Greg Gerik at 3M, his company was a strong and early adopter of forums to distribute insight more effectively across the entire enterprise. That dedication to strong, continuous communication has helped 3M avoid the split personality that can affect brands when only certain divisions or certain campaigns are backed by comprehensive and coordinated customer insights. Every stakeholder in 3M is empowered and encouraged to take part in the flow of information coming into 3M through its many engagement channels. "Many companies look at social in the enterprise as a function of communications, or IT, or marketing. The way we look at it, everybody should be concerned about the customer," Gerik says.[2]

Internal social collaboration is too broad a topic to cover in this book, but it is very important that you appreciate the dramatic productivity benefits of modern collaboration platforms and find the right one for your program.

Coach

The employees who participate in your social empowerment program will need to possess a wide range of skills and knowledge for engaging in social media. Some of your deepest internal experts may have no knowledge of how to engage in social media, whereas others may be early adopters who are highly active and already developing significant advocacy in external audiences.

One of the most effective and efficient ways to help your people advance their skills is to create a structure that lets people mentor and coach each other. Some brands officially designate internal coaches. That approach allows you to ensure that the coaches' managers support the effort, and everyone involved is able to allocate sufficient time and attention to make it successful.

You may also want to consider reverse mentoring, in which junior employees—often called *digital natives*—partner with a more senior leader who learns from the junior employee. The junior employees share their expertise in emerging technologies from a consumer's perspective. In exchange, the senior leader mentors the digital native to help them develop their career within the organization. Jack Welch instituted a program like this for his senior executives in the late 1990s when he realized that the Internet would be critical to GE's business, and many organizations have used this approach with success.[11]

Coaching is one of the best ways to ensure that your people stay engaged, and engaged workers are happier, more productive, and more enthusiastic about their work.

Your coaching effort should continually help employees to grow their professional brand, including goals like:

- Broadening their reach and visibility among the community of people who share their interests
- Effectively participating and engaging in meaningful, collaborative relationships in which they provide value to their customers, audiences, and communities
- Growing the level of engagement the employee achieves within their audience
- Nurturing advocacy within their audience (see Chapter 3, Influence: It's Complicated, for definitions of *advocacy* and *engagement*)
- Evolving and enhancing their skills in the technologies and platforms that can help them to achieve the above goals

In Chapter 4, The Power to Sway, we explain how to help employees develop advocacy online, and coaching is a big part of that. In particular, coaching should help employees find and nurture the topics and interests about which they feel passionate. Then, you should coach them to communicate with that passion in a way that suits their personality as well as their audience.

Measure Performance

Measurement is described in detail in Chapter 5.

---

11. Slater, Robert. *Jack Welch and the G.E. Way: Management Insight and Leadership Secrets of the Legendary CEO.* New York: McGraw-Hill, 1998.

Reward

Rewards and recognition are critical to the success of a social empowerment program. According to a 2012 study by the Society for Human Resource Management and Globoforce,[12] organizations with strategic recognition programs enjoy the following benefits, versus companies without such programs.

1. 28.6 percent lower frustration is exhibited.
2. Employees are 25.4 percent more likely to have a clear understanding of organizational objectives.
3. Employees feel 21.5 percent more enabled to help achieve organizational objectives.
4. The mean employee turnover rate is 23.4 percent lower.

And there are three critical elements in the recognition programs that achieve these kinds of results. First, each recognition moment should tie to organizational core values and strategic goals. Second, you must measure, record, and analyze the activity that is rewarded to continually improve the program. Third, you must apply consistent rewards to everyone in the program and centralize reporting to ensure consistency and efficiency throughout.

Before you begin looking for people to join the program, be sure to clarify what's in it for them. Determine whether their participation will affect their compensation—in the short term, via money, and in the long run, via career development and advancement. Help them understand the value to the business, so that they understand their contribution. Many people feel a sense of reward from knowing they are supporting the growth of the organization. Figure 2.7 shows examples of rewards that organizations have given employees.

In general, you should consult your Human Resources organization to determine the best mix of rewards and incentives for your organization, but we suggest at least considering the following types of rewards and recognition in your program, also illustrated in Figure 2.7.

- **Awards:** Awards are physical objects, visible to the people around them, that are given employees as symbols of their achievement. Examples in the physical world include a trophy or a certificate.

---

12. The Society for Human Resource Management and Globoforce. "Employee Recognition Survey—Fall 2012 Report: The Business Impact of Employee Recognition." Fall 2012. http://bit.ly/globo-survey.

Cash awards or points that accumulate and can be redeemed for prizes can also be interesting to employees. As the concept of *gamification*[13] proliferates enterprise applications, you should also consider virtual goods and badges. When Hugh McColl was CEO of NationsBank, his experience as a military officer was an important part of his professional persona, and, when employees achieved significant impact for the bank, he would visit their offices and roll a hand grenade made of crystal under their desk. If you run a collaboration platform for your employees, you might consider different badges for people to display their accomplishments to their peers.

- **Impacts on Job Role:** These are interesting because some of the examples are negative, and you may not want to go that direction. Stay positive. Provide coaches who help people grow their careers. Include social engagement goals to ensure that managers give people time and support to achieve them and do not to punish people who miss the target.

  Some employees may want to see how their participation helps them get promoted, and, in many organizations, that linkage may not exist. Specifically, the skills required for success in social media may not help an employee succeed as a manager or executive. You need to be honest with yourself and your employees about the extent to which their participation can help them advance their careers.

- **Professional Recognition:** Think of ways to elevate the status of employees among their professional peers—beyond their immediate team and the people they encounter on a daily basis.

- **External Recognition:** Think of ways to help employees grow their reputations and increase their ability to influence or develop relationships through digital and in-person activities. Examples can include listing a certification on their business card, placing a branded icon on their personal Web site, or featuring them in branded promotions and brand Web content.

---

13. *Gamification* is the use of constructs or rules that produce a game-like atmosphere to increase the levels of engagement of people within a system, but not necessarily increase their fun.

Example Rewards or Links to Career		Example Benefits Expected
Awards	• Certificate or trophy • Badge on internal profile	• Tangible rewards for achieving certifications at each level
Impacts on Job Role	• Deadlines to complete certification following completion of courses • Manager notified on certification failure • Add to Career Development Plan • Add to Personal Goals for the performance year • Coaches serve as a resource for individuals going through certification	• Career advancement • Encourages individuals to take certification process seriously • Identifies individuals that may not be in the right role • Coaches mentor individual employees through certification and subsequent development
Professional Recognition	• Certified club or community of practice • All Hands recognition • Announcement in internal newsletter	• Provides recognition internally among peers and leadership
External Recognition	• Certification level indicated on business cards • Profile on brand Web site, (e.g., adjacent to product information that is relevant to the employee) • Feature in digital promotions for brand events	• Provides differentiation from peers

Figure 2.7 *Example reward structure for a social empowerment program*

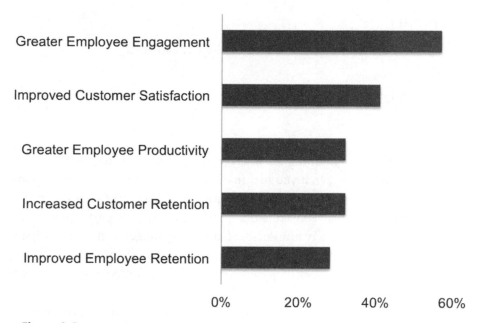

Figure 2.8 *Share of HR managers who perceived each benefit after implementing a peer-to-peer recognition program*

Source: The Society for Human Resource Management and Globoforce. "Employee Recognition Survey—Fall 2012 Report: The Business Impact of Employee Recognition." Fall 2012. http://bit.ly/globo-survey.

Within your reward program, also consider the potential value of peer-to-peer rewards. According to the Society for Human Resources Management, 812 surveyed HR leaders believe that, after implementing peer-to-peer recognition programs, companies achieved greater employee engagement (see Figure 2.8).

Finally, as stated by Alex Laurs who leads development of training and rewards programs for clients of Accenture:

> When designing any system of rewards or incentives, it's important to clearly define the behavior(s) you're looking to drive and the outcomes you expect the rewards to achieve for the business. You need to ensure that you clarify how the program will pay for itself. Then, run a pilot to test the business case, and refine the reward structure accordingly.[14]

---

14. Laurs, Alex. Personal interview. January 2013.

Transition

Activities during the Transition stage include the following:

1. Succession
2. Turnover

Succession

Succession involves planning for when your employees need to leave your program and ensuring that you identify new people to take over the responsibilities of departing employees. Some employees may leave your company, or they may move to another role that prevents them from participating in the program. Or they may just decide that they no longer wish to participate.

In any case, you should determine how you will handle departures of the most critical employees that you empower in social media, such as your thought leaders.

In most cases, it is very difficult to quickly replace one employee with another. In this regard, it's a lot like a sales organization that relies on strong client relationships to sell. It takes time for new employees to learn everything they need to know and to establish relationships with external audiences that will help them to succeed. Therefore, you must continually cultivate the next generation of socially empowered employees.

It will be critical to the long-term success of your program to continually identify new employees who will become future thought leaders. Give them some level of coaching and feedback, and let them know that you want them to be thought leaders in the future. Then they will be there when you need them.

Turnover

When employees leave your program, you will want to ensure that you preserve as much of the assets and knowledge they created as you can. If you implemented an effective knowledge management system, this should not be a big effort. Things you will want to do are listed in the example employee exit checklist for a social employee enablement program illustrated in Figure 2.9.

In anticipation of employees leaving, you should specify who owns the assets they create according to some agreement that is clear to the employees. If you try to make everything they create a corporate asset, you will not be able to attract the best people. So, you need to find a balance that works for

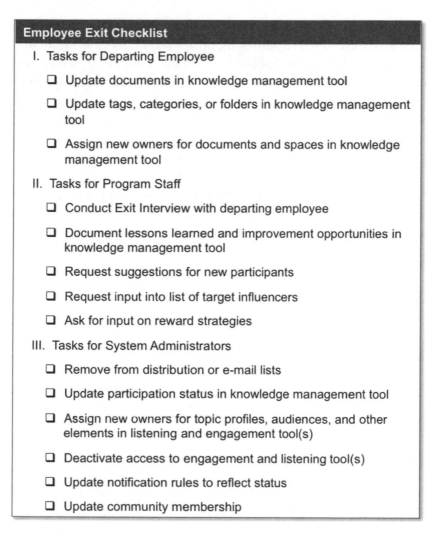

Figure 2.9 *Example employee exit checklist*

your brand and your people. This topic is best addressed through collaboration with your legal counsel.

Also, specify when social media accounts are owned by the employee and when they are owned by the brand. Do this as soon as you bring any employee into the program.

At a company by the name of Phonedog, a contract employee had established a Twitter account at the request of the brand. When he terminated his employment with the brand, he took the account with him, by changing the *handle* on the account. The parties dispute the sequence of events, but the contractor said he changed the "@PhoneDog_Noah" username to "@noahkravitz" with PhoneDog's blessing. PhoneDog sued in July 2011, demanding significant monetary compensation from the contractor and asserting claims for conversion, misappropriation of trade secrets, and interference with economic relationships. The case was due to proceed in court. Then, in December 2012, the parties settled, and the contractor retained the Twitter account.[15]

When you empower employees in social media, the whole point is to mix the personal reputation and audience of the employee with goals of the brand. Separating the two defeats the entire purpose. So, you need to establish clear agreements with your employees at the beginning of your effort. Always.

Optimize

Measurement is described in Chapter 5.

Lead

When you empower employees in social media, many of your managers will need to change their perspectives and opinions about how employees are allowed to participate online.

Overcome the Loss of Control

In many companies, employee participation in social media is still taboo. As described in IBM's study, "The Business of Social Business: What Works and How It's Done," a disconnect exists in many organizations between the senior executives who see the value in applying social capabilities and the managers who must embrace these capabilities as part of their day-to-day work. While 48 percent of organizations indicated that they have support from the C-Suite, only 22 percent believed that managers are prepared to incorporate social business into their daily practices.[16]

---

15. Balasubramani, Venkat. "Employee/Ex-Employer Lawsuit Over Twitter Account Settles—Phonedog v. Kravitz." *Technology & Marketing Law Blog.* 4 December 2012. http://bit.ly/PhoneDog-Case.

16. Cortada, James W., Eric Lesser, and Peter J. Korsten. "The Business of Social Business: What Works and How It's Done." IBM Institute for Business Value, 2012. http://bit.ly/ibm_social.

Andrew McAfee, a Principal Research Scientist from the MIT Center for Digital Business, who was interviewed for the study, stated in a *Sloan Management Review* interview[17]:

> When I talk to CEO's, they desperately want to hear the voices of their customers, the voices of their employees . . . But I get the impression that there is a middle layer that traditionally has been the signal processor, both up and down, and some of them don't want to see that role go away.

Simply stated, empowering employees in social media makes many managers uncomfortable; they feel a loss of control, and they don't like that.

One way that successful social brands overcome this is to think about roles such as sales people or customer service agents who talk to customers or prospects all day. Managers of sales and customer service teams do not preapprove everything the employees say to every customer and prospect; that kind of approach would never scale. Instead, the managers provide training, coaching, content, and periodic spot checks.

The same is true when empowering employees in social media. The difference is that more of your employees will have more interactions with more external audiences, online and in public. So, your people will need new skills, education and training, guidance, and ongoing support on how to effectively engage with their intended audience. And that is what managers are supposed to do.

Figure 2.10 shows some of the topics that you will need to demonstrate, explain, or prove to managers, as well as some of the topics that you will need to help employees address with their managers.

Tear Down That Wall[18]

One of the most established and ingrained assumptions in modern organizations is the idea that there should be a very hard boundary between the communications that go outside of the organization and any internal communications and collaboration. This stems partially from conventional wisdom that organizations should be broken into sets of internal functions such as sales, marketing, or HR, and that responsibilities for communication

---

17. Kiron, David. "What Sells CEOs on Social Networking." *MIT Sloan Management Review.* 7 February 2012. http://bit.ly/SloanMcafee.
18. Adapted from the famous declaration by Ronald Reagan at the Brandenburg Gate in Berlin, Germany, on 12 June 1987.

Managers Need to Feel Comfortable That...	Employees Will Want Their Manager to Know...
• Employee time in social media helps meet my team goals, as well as individual employee goals	• The ways that people communicate have changed
• Employees are familiar with and following brand social policies and guidelines	• The way I interact online is personal and authentic to me
• Social interactions support business goals (e.g., demand generation or customer service)	• I don't have time to participate everywhere; I need to focus on high value opportunities
• Employees recognize that they represent the brand	• I recognize that my interactions and relationships with customers, prospects and peers influence opinions
• Employees feel confident that we are here to support them	• I am part of a network and I have the potential to influence customers if supported effectively
• Employees are willing to share information about our brand	• I can provide an authentic, authoritative voice, and I can proactively influence perceptions of our brand and products

Figure 2.10 *Concerns for managers and employees to address during recruiting and onboarding*

should be divided according to constituencies, such as customers, investors, governments, the media, and communities.

While that approach fits neatly into an org chart, that is not how human networks work. Instead, people naturally form social networks when they share a relationship or a common interest. The network of relationships between people in a social network is often called a *social graph*. In general, we find it helpful to consider the following two types of social graphs, which vary according to the nature of the relationships between the people in the network.

Networks that form around personal relationships are often referred to as a *relationship graph,* where people connect because they work together, have attended the same school, are part of a family, or have some other kind of relationship. LinkedIn, in its early days, was mostly a relationship graph where people connected because they already knew each other through a work-related relationship.

Networks that form around topical interests are often referred to as an *interest graph,* where people connect to each other because they want to know about or discuss a topic even though they may have no other relationship. Twitter is an example of an interest graph network, where people often *follow* each other based on interests alone.

Social networks do not form along the lines of internal and external organizational boundaries. So, when you empower your people in social media, don't let organizational boundaries get in the way of people joining your program. It does not matter which organizations they work in; what matters is whether they can add value to your program. When bringing together internal experts, let people organize according to their interests, regardless of where they sit in the company.

Many managers subconsciously appreciate internal silos and external segment definitions because they help to maintain clear lines of control; however, in the modern social business, those structures clash.

The IT department might try to enforce such boundaries in the name of information security, but it's a losing battle. Instead, organizations must honor the nature of interpersonal networks while also ensuring information security. That requires new approaches and new tools, some of which we discuss in Chapter 6.

Instead of working to strengthen such boundaries, brands can create significantly greater value by extending and integrating their capabilities beyond organizational boundaries. In the 1980s and '90s, many people referred to this idea as "the networked enterprise." While economists debated the extent to which gains from then-emerging Web technologies actually increased productivity, McKinsey stated in 2010 that companies that use "collaborative Web 2.0 technologies intensively to connect the internal efforts of employees and to extend the organization's reach to customers, partners, and suppliers are not only more likely to be market leaders or to be gaining market share but also use management practices that lead to margins higher than those of companies using the Web in more limited ways."[19]

Empowering employees in social media advances the *networked enterprise* concept to its next logical stage of development, where brands unleash the power in the social networks of their employees.

Managers who get on board will lead their organizations into the future.

Here are two examples of how you can ensure that organizational boundaries stay out of the way:

- **Collaboration Platform:** Provide software tools that enable people to share information and content across the organization, regardless of organizational boundaries. Products in this category include Jive, IBM Connections, Salesforce Chatter, Igloo, Yammer, and Share-Point. Although those are the typical solutions deployed at large companies, there are many other tools that provide more specialized functionality or focus more on serving smaller companies.

- **Focus on Content Availability:** Too many organizations place control of their content into the hands of a few select people—usually marketers and professional communicators. And they make it very difficult for employees to find or use the content via social media. Instead, you should strive to make content and digital assets more available to employees. Make it easy for employees to find great content and share it with their audiences. Make it easy for your people to find answers to the questions about your brand that they encounter when dialoguing with external audiences online.

Over time, marketing, PR, and brand must shift some of their efforts from directing assets and communications to empowering others to communicate and to create valuable content that more employees and partners can use. The brands that do so will win in the market.

How Social Brands Tend to Evolve

When you begin to plan the services you will provide to employees that you enable in social media, you will need to align your plans with your organization's

---

19. Bughin, Jacques, and Chui, Michael. "The Rise of the Networked Enterprise: Web 2.0 Finds Its Payday." *McKinsey Quarterly.* McKinsey & Company, December 2010. http://bit.ly/McKinsey-Networked.

Ad Hoc	Experimenting	Scaling
Typical Social Employees		
Early Adopters	Fast Followers	Broad Workforce
Motivations of Social Employees		
Curiosity, Desire to Lead	Evidence of Other's Success	Official Encouragement or Job Requirement
Brand Capabilities		
• Limited or no executive support or funding	• Funded program manager(s)	• Experts aligned to business priorities
• Employees use social media in their spare time	• Capability road map	• Deployment across business units and functions
• Free tools, selected by each employee	• Initial deployment to a business unit or function	• Model behaviors defined
• People may attend webinars for education	• Relationship management siloed between PR or brand management and the social employee program	• Digital asset repository
	• Self-serve training and education	• Relationship tracking tool
	• Deliberate enablement of high-profile or deeply knowledgeable experts	• Employee success metrics
	• Personalized training and coaching for select employees	• Collaboration between marketers & employees
		• Content developed for the employee channel

Figure 2.11 *Evolution of the social brand capabilities*

maturity in social media and your maturity in social employee empowerment. In general, the level of support that a brand provides to employees usually follows three broad stages of evolution, as shown in Figure 2.11.

In the beginning, early adopters sprinkled across the company begin to use social media on their own. They receive limited support from the brand, and probably no funding. They use free tools in their spare time, and they might attend webinars or local free conferences[20] to connect with other people with similar interests in using social media for business. Individuals are experimenting, but the organization is not. We call this stage *Ad Hoc*.

---

20. See meetup.com for opportunities like this.

In the second stage of development, experimentation moves from the individual level to the organizational level. At this stage, *fast followers* see the *early adopters* having some success, and they begin to follow. At this point, the organization gives someone accountability for enabling some set of employees in social media. They are officially spending money on it. There may be a road map for developing the capabilities needed for success, but the scope is usually limited to one business unit or functional team, such as marketing or customer service. Training is usually self-serve for most employees, via the employee portal or an internal microsite. Select employees get a higher level of support and maybe some personalized training or coaching.

In the third stage of evolution, which we call *Scaling*, the organization buys into the power of enabling employees in social media and scales capabilities across the organization. Most of the work force is encouraged and supported to engage in social media. In addition, experts are aligned to business priorities and probably even partner with product marketers to support marketing programs and editorial calendars. Metrics for success are defined and regularly assessed for each employee who is a subject matter expert or thought leader. Employees participate because their manager encourages it and, in some cases, social media engagement is required for their job. Finally, the organization develops content specifically for distribution through employees in social media. And they even measure the performance of that content.

Your Next Steps

1. Determine the extent to which employees already publish in social media in ways that support their online influence or credibility around topics that the brand cares about.
2. Determine criteria that employees should meet to be empowered in social media. You might create tiers: one for all employees and another for experts.
3. Start a list of potential program candidates.
4. For a set of employees whom you might empower in social media, determine their current skills and any new skills they may need to learn.
5. Determine your organization's requirements for training. Assess capabilities for developing a training curriculum and certification program.

3

Influence: It's Complicated

Coauthored by Constantin Basturea

"[W]hat makes social media powerful. . . . [I]t's the cumulative effect of many people, some of whom are influential broadly, but many who are influential specifically to you, and the sum of their experiences that weigh upon your mind."

— Christopher S. Penn

Many brands invest time and money into relationships with online influencers. The most successful influencer relationship programs spread their efforts across a wider portfolio of influencers and also invest in helping employees establish their own influence, at many different levels.

As stated in 2011 by Matt Monahan, a highly successful investor in social advertising start-ups,

> The social web has democratized influence and diluted its primary motive. The previous motive was to get legacy media paid-laid-made. Influence is now used (more purely) to create revolution, educate, entertain, drive culture, build brands and (even) sell products.[1]

In the early days of social media, many people mistakenly thought that social media success could be achieved by identifying the few people who exert the most influence in online conversations about your brand or category, then building relationships with them so that you could get them to say nice things about your brand, or at least prevent them from publishing statements that were not true.

Still today, *influencer relations* receive a great deal of attention and consume significant energy within many brands because of the promise of achieving a great result: influencing large numbers of people by persuading a small number of individuals, usually known as *influencers*.

As stated by Dr. Michael Wu, Principal Scientist of Analytics at Lithium, "Influencer marketing provides brands with the leverage to reach many by engaging only a few elusive influencers."[2] This is often called the *influencer hypothesis*.[3]

The Nature of Online Influence Is Often Misunderstood

The reality of online and offline influence is a bit more nuanced.

On one side of the debate, research conducted by Dr. Duncan Watts (a principal researcher at Microsoft Research) and his associates shows that the influencer hypothesis doesn't hold water.[4]

---

1. Dubois, Lou. "Why Social Influence Matters to Businesses." 31 March 2011. http://bit.ly/InfluenceMatters. Matt Monahan invested in Wildfire, which was acquired by Google, and is a mentor at 500 Hats. At the time of Dubois' article, Matt Monahan was Director of Social Media at EpicSocial.
2. Wu, Michael. "The Problem with Measuring Digital Influence." *TechCrunch.* 19 November 2012.
3. The term *influencer hypothesis* was coined by Duncan Watts in "Challenging the Influentials Hypothesis." *Measuring Word of Mouth,* vol. 3. Chicago, IL: Word of Mouth Marketing Association, 2007.
4. Watts, Duncan J. *Everything Is Obvious: *Once You Know the Answer.* New York: Crown Business, 2011, 94-7. See also: Watts, Duncan J., and Peter Sheridan Dodds. "Influentials, Networks, and Public Opinion Formation." *Journal of Consumer Research,* 34, no. 4 (2007):441-58.

Watts began by performing computer simulations which showed that, "under most conditions, highly influential individuals were indeed more effective than the average person in triggering social epidemics," but far less effective than expected.

Instead, when trying to influence a large number of people via a small number of people, the nature of the target publics matters more than any attributes of the potential influencers. Specifically, Dr. Watts discovered that the existence of ". . . a critical mass of easily influenced people who influence other easy-to-influence people. . ." was more important for triggering social contagion than influencers' contributions.

Subsequent research on a real-world social network confirmed the results. After analyzing 74 million cascades of tweets (meaning, tweets and their subsequent chains of retweets), Watts found that,

> . . . on average, individuals with many followers who had been successful at triggering cascades of retweets in the past were more likely to be successful in the future . . .[5]

However, he also found that no one person on Twitter was sufficiently reliable in their ability to create significant cascades of tweets, or, as many would say, to influence the conversation on Twitter. In fact, Watts suggested that,

> marketing strategies that focus on targeting a few 'special' individuals are bound to be unreliable . . . therefore, marketers should adopt a portfolio approach, targeting a large number of potential influencers and harnessing their average effect. . .[5]

Advertising industry researchers like Ed Keller, CEO of The Keller Fay Group, have said that Watts' findings miss the mark, stating "If I had $100 to spend, and I could spend it focusing on the mass market or I could put some chips on a group that could get me somewhere between two and five times as much energy with word of mouth, well, they're going to get my message out more quickly and more efficiently."[6]

---

5. Watts, Duncan J. *Everything Is Obvious: *Once You Know the Answer.* New York: Crown Business, 2011, 98–105. See also: Bakshy, Eytan, Jake Hofman, Winter A. Mason, and Duncan J. Watts. "Everyone's an Influencer: Quantifying Influence on Twitter." *Proceedings of the 4th International Conference on Web Search and Data Mining, Hong Kong, 2011.*
6. Thompson, Clive. "Is the Tipping Point Toast?" *Fast Company.* 1 February 2008. http://bit.ly/ TippingToast.

However, Keller also said that, ". . . nobody, including myself, thinks that Influencers are the only group of consumers who matter."[6]

Virality versus Homophily

Research by Sinan Aral et al.[7] at the Stern School of Business at NYU suggests that more than 50 percent of product adoption behavior that we perceive as viral actually may occur because the people in the network simply have a lot in common; and less than 50 percent of the perceived viral product adoption occurs because of what we commonly think of as *influence.*

In other words, when people connect on a social network, they tend to connect because of a shared interest or some common attributes, and that commonality causes those connected people to adopt similar products. To say it another way, Professor Aral's research[7] indicates that most viral product adoption may occur simply because people who adopt new products through viral mechanisms are simply alike in many ways or have some common interest.

Along that point, Chris Penn warns, "Think carefully about what makes social media powerful. It isn't just people with high Klout scores. It's the cumulative effect of many people, some of whom are influential broadly, but many who are influential specifically to you, and the sum of their experiences that weigh upon your mind."[8]

And that is why online communities can be very powerful: they concentrate people according to a shared interest. In fact, online communities that bring together people with common interests are often more powerful than individuals whom we typically consider to be influencers.

Velvet Rope Communities

To further illustrate this point, Chris Penn talks about *velvet rope communities,* which can be online or offline communities whose membership is controlled and usually private. Membership is not available to the general public,

---

7. Aral, Sinan, Lev Muchnik, and Arun Sundararajan. "Distinguishing Influence-Based Contagion from Homophily-Driven Diffusion in Dynamic Networks." *Proceedings of the National Academy of Sciences.* 2009. http://www.pnas.org/content/early/2009/12/09/0908800106.
8. Henley, Brett. "Top Influence Marketing News—The Future of Influencer Analytics." 24 August 2012. http://bit.ly/InfluenceNews.

and most people probably don't even know the group exists. Chris provides the following example:

> In the martial arts world, Stephen K. Hayes is a legend. He heads up a network of martial arts practitioners that number in the thousands across the world, and when he speaks in the organization's private, invisible-to-Google forums, everyone pays attention. Yet if you plug his name or information into any of the standard "influence metrics" available to marketers and public relations specialists, you'd likely give him a miss. His Klout score is below 40, which wouldn't even qualify him for your standard Klout perk, but he could easily mobilize hundreds of people to your cause if you had access to his velvet rope community.[9]

Traditional influencer identification would never identify or have any effectiveness in this kind of velvet rope community. If you want to develop relationships with these kinds of highly influential groups, your employees will need to join and engage as invited members. That means the employees who participate must do so because they have a genuine interest in the topic, and not because they were given an assignment to build a relationship.

To summarize, there are a few takeaways when we consider influencer relations in the context of employee enablement.

- People who have shown the ability to influence in the past are more likely than average to be able to influence in the future.

- However, no one does it consistently, so you need a portfolio of influencers.

- To a degree, influence is personal. People are more likely to connect with people like them and are more likely to be influenced to share information or adopt products by people like them, not by "influencers."

- Not all influencers are easy to spot. Velvet rope communities often exert significant influence, but they are difficult to identify. Further, such private communities may be led or influenced heavily by people who do not appear in traditional influencer research or social network analyses.

Given the above sources of influence, brands that want to develop and nurture relationships with external influencers and advocates should use a

---

9. Penn, Christopher S. "The Danger of the Single Influencer." SHIFT Communications. 7 December 2012. http://bit.ly/SingleInfluencer.

distributed approach to outreach and relationship development. That means you will probably need relationships with more "influencers" and "communities" than you nurture today.

It also means that you may need to empower more diverse people from your brand to develop those relationships and engage in those communities. In general, a distributed, portfolio approach becomes easier and more effective when you empower more people, such as employees and business partners, to establish and maintain those relationships.

How Social Employees Empower Brands

Employees can help support relationships with influencers and communities through a wide range of activities and at many different levels of effect. In the next two sections we present a couple of examples.

Example: Dion Hinchcliffe, Dachis Group

At the broadest level of impact, employees can earn high notoriety or fame by publishing their knowledge and expertise through traditional, established media as well as social media. Such traditional media could include interviews in professional journals, appearances on television talk shows, and articles featured in major news publications. Employees who are able to distribute their point of view through mainstream media can establish trust and credibility with very large audiences and can significantly affect brand reputation online and off.

As an example, consider Dion Hinchcliffe at Dachis Group. Dion joined Dachis Group when they acquired a company that he founded. At the time, Dion had established a large following in social media and had published significantly in traditional media. As part of his company's acquisition, Dion established an agreement with the CEO of Dachis Group, Jeff Dachis, that Dion would continue to publish his personal points of view, as he had always done.

Since joining Dachis Group, Dion has continued to publish through *ZDNet* and *InformationWeek,* which are traditional publishers in the technology industry, with significant audiences. Dion also publishes his own blog,[10] writes on the Dachis Group blog,[11] and published a book in 2012 with Peter Kim,[12] also of the Dachis Group.

As a result of publishing through traditional media and social media, Dion has established a global following of senior executives and decision makers around the world and is widely recognized as an authority in his field. Without a doubt, Dion would be considered an "influencer" by most definitions and most influencer-identification systems. Benefits to Dachis Group include greater awareness of their brand and their offerings, increased consideration of their organization for the services they provide, and increased ability to sell their professional services, which require their clients to rely upon the expertise of people like Dion.

Example: Willie Favero, IBM

Many brands enjoy the benefits of people known as *thought leaders,* who publish ideas that help other people solve problems or achieve their goals. They may not be celebrities in their field, but they consistently publish content that advances their field. Examples could include senior executives at consultancies who publish primary research or books, or a professional chef who publishes recipes that include the brand's food products.

Willie Favero of IBM is a leader in Data Warehousing on System z, and he writes a blog on that topic. And although the general public may have no idea what that means, there are a lot of people with an interest in DB2 and mainframe computers who know Willie Favero very well. At least, they know him through his online reputation very well.

Willie attracts more than 6,000 RSS subscribers and more than 15,000 visitors per month to his blog. In addition, he is often quoted by industry professionals, such as one presenter at a large industry conference who said, "I picked up this item in my presentation from Willie's blog."[13]

---

10. http://dionhinchcliffe.com
11. http://bit.ly/Dion-Blog
12. Hinchcliffe, Dion, and Peter Kim. *Social Business by Design: Transformative Social Media Strategies for the Connected Company.* San Francisco, CA: Jossey-Bass, 2012.
13. Emerick, Susan. "A Chat with Willie Favero DB2 for z/OS Evangelist about His Secrets for Social Media Success." http://SusanEmerick.com. 1 May 2012.

Willie's blog also caught the eye of his manager, who understood the value of sharing expertise with a dedicated following, so they mutually agreed to include engagement in social media into his performance plan. In our discussions with Willie, he remarked, "I like having my manager's buy-in because it takes the pressure off my blogging activity and I'm recognized for it. Everyone active in social media should get that same support."

B2C EXAMPLE: EMPOWERING EMPLOYEES TO SUPPORT A TIRE BRAND

A global tire brand had been focusing its social media efforts on connecting with influencers on two well-known social media venues: Facebook and Twitter. Their brand-owned accounts and their handful of socially engaged employees published content, shared information, and answered customer questions fairly actively in those two venues. Yet, the brand had not achieved significant business results from their efforts. Why?

After researching the online venues where customers discussed the brands products—and those of its competitors—the brand discovered that most of their customers did not discuss their tires on Facebook and Twitter. Instead, the majority of online conversations about tires occurred in online forums. It is within these forums that the brand discovered the most influential thought leaders conducting and actively responding to discussions. The brand had been engaging in the wrong places.

Initially, the brand considered shifting its social media resources toward the online forums where customers discussed their products, but such a strategy would have proven impossible, for two reasons.

First, discussion about tires is spread across a large number of forums, and each forum is focused on a specific car brand. For example, BMW owners tend to discuss tires on forums dedicated to BMW owners, and Corvette owners tend to discuss tires on forums dedicated to Corvette owners. Therefore, the brand would need to engage within a large number of forums.

Second, the consumers in those forums only engage with people who earn their trust and respect as people who are (1) knowledgeable about the cars and (2) sincere in the statements that they post. The people in those forums know each other, especially the leading influencers who are tightly connected. They see each other at events in person. Credibility is not something that can be faked on online car forums.

Because of the two above factors, it would have been physically impossible for a small team of marketers to cover the required number of car forums with the necessary levels of expertise and commitment to establish any degree of influence.

Instead, the brand decided to equip a select set of employees who had a combination of product knowledge and sincere domain interest to build relationships within select forums. The employees were supported by the marketing organization, which provided content and access to internal tire product experts with specialized expertise.

The select employees were sent to events attended by forum participants, where the employees could develop in-person relationships with the people who influenced conversations in the online forums. Over time, the employees build credibility for themselves and, subsequently, for their brand.

Distributed Public Relations

In addition to employees who focus significant time and energy into developing content and relationships, many more of your employees or partners can establish relationships with people outside of the brand. In general, you can think of this model as a form of *distributed public relations,* where you empower internal experts to develop and maintain relationships with people outside of your brand who have or could have an interest in your brand.

This kind of approach was described by Tom Kelleher as ". . . the intentional practice of sharing public relations responsibilities among a broad cross section of an organization's members or employees, particularly in an online context."[14]

When Duncan Watts analyzed the cost-benefit trade-offs of buying express support from well-established influencers on Twitter, he found that individuals who exhibit average or even less-than-average influence often proved to be the most cost-effective channel to disseminate information. Meaning, it is possible to get more value for your dollar if you focus on influencing people with lower levels of influence.

And that brings us to another way of empowering employees to support brand goals through their social media. Many of your employees can simply establish their presence online and develop relationships with audiences who have an interest in the employee's domain of expertise. In this case, the size of the audience really does not matter.

---

14. Kelleher, Tom. *Public Relations Online: Lasting Concepts for Changing Media.* Thousand Oaks, CA: SAGE Publications, Inc., 2006, 98.

DISTRIBUTED PUBLIC RELATIONS THROUGH TRADITIONAL CHANNELS

In the world of customer relationship management (CRM), Paul Greenberg is a world-famous consultant and writer. He advises the world's largest software brands, and many smaller brands, too. He coined the term *social CRM,* and his book, *CRM at the Speed of Light,*[15] is recognized as a landmark in the development of modern CRM concepts. Nearly everyone in the world of CRM knows the name Paul Greenberg.

In March 2010, Joe Hughes of Accenture wrote an article, which Paul then reviewed on his Web site. In his usual candor, Paul made it clear that it was a good start, but he expected more from Accenture.[16]

So, Joe reached out to Paul. They spoke.

Anyone who knows Paul will tell you that he does not hold back. If you ask for his opinion, he'll give it to you straight. And that was exactly what he did.

And Joe listened. He didn't defend. He didn't explain. He listened. He took Paul's feedback, and then he acted on it. Between 2010 and 2012, Joe and Paul developed a trust-based relationship that today supports open dialog and information exchange on behalf of the Accenture brand. And that relationship has played a role in helping Accenture—through Joe and his team—to refine their points of view and market positioning in social CRM.

Throughout their relationship, Paul and Joe typically interact through traditional channels, such as e-mail, phone, and in-person meetings. So, employees can use traditional channels to nurture external relationships. You don't have to focus exclusively on social media, and you probably should not focus in that way. What matters is that employees are taking on responsibilities that historically belonged to PR and marketing professionals. In fact, ten years ago, it only would have been Forrester and an Analyst Relations person interacting.

Social media made this relationship possible in two ways. First, if not for social media, Paul would not have had the tools to establish such influence and presence. Social media empowered him to become an influencer in a way that historically was reserved for journalists.

Second, social media have forever changed our expectations about regular employees publishing and establishing relationships with influencers. These days, it is perfectly normal for some of your employees to become famous thought leaders using only their own resources, and it's common practice for someone like Joe Hughes to reach out to a blogger like Paul, on his own, without a team of media relations staff managing the process.

---

15. Greenberg, Paul. *CRM at the Speed of Light.* Berkeley, CA: Osborne McGraw-Hill, 2001.
16. Greenberg, Paul. "Aggregating Some Random Pieces: The Social CRM 'Industry.'" PGreenblog.com. 8 March 2010. http://bit.ly/RandomPaul.

Benefits of Empowering More Employees in Social Media

There are three primary reasons for empowering employees in social media in this way: inbound links, social signals in search engines, and trust in "someone like me."

First, inbound links in social media and mentions in social media can improve your performance in search engine results. In fact, inbound links in social media are a top driver of search engine placement, as we explained in Chapter 1, Web of Trust: The Case for the Social Work Force. If your employees create lots of inbound links to your content in their social media, that will help your performance in search engines.

Second, if you are logged in when you search on Google, you can see results from people in your social network. So, if employees link to your content in their personal social media, then the people in their online networks are likely to see that linked content in their search results.

Third, as explained in Chapter 1, people are most likely to trust "someone like me." Edelman's most recent Trust Barometer ranked "technical expert inside the company" as the most credible internal spokesperson for the last few years, and that trust continues to rise. In 2011, it was 64 percent. In 2012 it climbed to 66 percent.

Even a *regular employee* is trusted more than the CEO. Trust in CEOs dropped 12 points in 2012—the biggest decline in the Barometer's history. Meanwhile, trust in the *regular employee* rose 16 points—the biggest increase since the 2004 study.

Ford Motor Company is one brand taking advantage of this ongoing shift in trust. As an example, Jim Farley, Chief Marketing and Sales Officer at Ford, described Ford's approach to their Drive One campaign, saying, "The first thing we did in Drive One was, we put our front line engineers to talk about the company, because they're believable." [17]

As you empower more of your employees in social media, you increase the diversity of people from your brand that you expose to external audiences. And there are lots of audiences, so there are lots of definitions of "someone like me." Luckily, your organization probably contains different types of employees and partners, with different areas of expertise, different

---

17. Farley, Jim. "Finding Authentic Stories." McKinsey Global Institute, 2011. http://bit.ly/AuthenticStories. Video.

personalities, and so on. Therefore, the goal is to help your employees connect and engage with people who are "like" them—ideally, in ways that support your business goals.

As a result, you dramatically increase the probability that people outside your brand will encounter "someone like them" mentioning your brand or sharing brand-related content in a way that they will find engaging and useful. This could include existing friends and family of your employees, but more importantly would include decision makers or those who influence decision makers in an area of priority to your brand. For many employees, this will also include people whom they meet through social media that share common interests and share knowledge in a professional context, as they build their personal presence over time.

Your Next Steps

1. Determine where you already have employees or thought leaders who have built an influential presence in social media, and determine how you can help them achieve even more impact.
2. Use the other chapters in this book to assess the opportunity for empowering more employees in social media, in the context of your business priorities.
3. Take a look at your existing influencer relationship activities, and see whether you might be too focused on too few influencers. Maybe you could grow the portfolio of influencers that you nurture.
4. Consider conducting research to better understand where influencers who are important to your brand are actually spending their time online. Determine whether you need to make adjustments to the venues where you engage.

The Power to Sway: Helping Employees Build Advocacy Online

Coauthored by Constantin Basturea

"You will get all you want in life if you help enough other people get what they want."

— Zig Ziglar

While many brands have given their employees permission to use social media on their own or on behalf of the brand, few brands support employees in a systematic framework to develop a web of trust relationships beyond the borders of the organization to support and protect the brand. This chapter provides a framework for such activity.

Permission Is Not Enough

In our experience with large and small brands, we have seen employees empowered in social media for a wide range of goals, such as the following:

- For a luxury brand, empowering employees in social media helps to develop stronger emotional ties between customers and the brand. The brand creates more dialogue with customers, which allows customers to feel like they are a part of the brand—that they're essentially on the inside. Subsequently, that helps to extend the luxury brand's ability to deliver an aspirational experience to their consumers.

- For a global retailer, the brand can initiate and participate in framing conversations about its products and services, as well as in industry debates and emerging issues, such as sustainability or diversity.

- A technology manufacturer can create an early warning system for product or service problems that will help it to increase satisfaction of customers and channel partners, while decreasing product, sales, and supply chain costs.

- Many brands more effectively absorb reputational shocks and mitigate crises when employees form a *web of trust* that includes external influencers and advocates.

If you believe in that potential, and you want to empower your employees to help achieve it, then you have to do more than simply tell them about your policies and give them permission to engage.

This chapter explains a structured approach for brands to systematically empower employees and partners. With this approach, your employees and partners can develop a web of trust, which is critical to achieving the kinds of goals that most brands seek to achieve, such as:

- Developing stronger emotional ties with customers
- Framing conversations or conditioning a market for products and services
- Improving customer services
- Supporting crisis management

How to Help Employees Build Online Advocacy

As we described in Chapter 1, Web of Trust: The Case for the Social Work Force, building trust and credibility online helps to increase one's influence, but trust and credibility must be earned over time, through active and sustained commitment to social engagement. You can't just decide to build influence, throw a pile of money at it, and get the result you want. In reality, you can only create conditions that are likely to lead to developing influence. Then you must let it evolve, with continual care and support.

Empowering employees and partners in social media is not simply a matter of using traditional influencer outreach with more people. Traditional PR approaches to influencer outreach simply do not work when you start adding lots of employees and partners into the process. In reality, including more people requires a different approach.

If you want to empower multiple employees to build advocacy for your brand, you'll need to provide a support structure for your employees—just as you would with any other organizational capability. Especially when your employees already have a full-time job. More than likely, most of your employees are not professional communicators.

In order to help you, we developed the following approach, based on our years of experience supporting influencer relationship programs in various industries.

The framework in Figure 4.1 shows the steps and activities required to help your employees establish trust, credibility, and influence online. The framework scales to organizations of all sizes. For a small company, each box could exist as one PowerPoint slide or checklist. For a global enterprise, each box could require multiple documents and a Web-based data repository or collaboration platform. We will describe each of them in detail in the remainder of this chapter.

Prepare

The Prepare phase helps you to clarify what you plan to achieve and how you plan to achieve it. In addition, you will clarify how you intend to measure your progress and the outcomes that you achieve through development

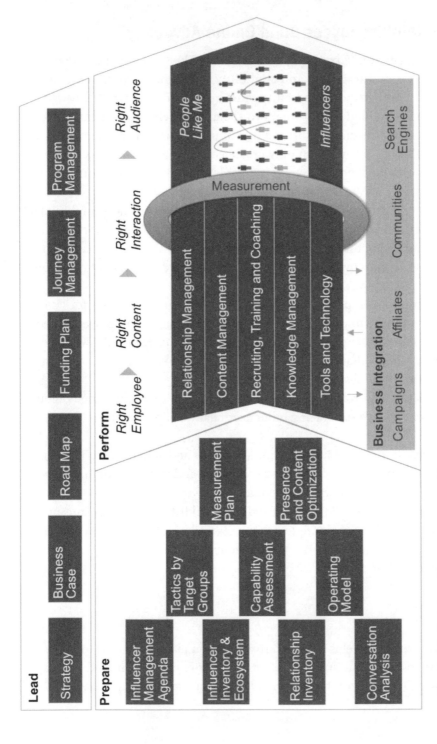

Figure 4.1 *Social employee empowerment framework*

of relationships with influencers. You begin by specifying what you want to achieve for your organization in the Influencer Management agenda.

Influencer Management Agenda

The Influencer Management agenda defines your goals for Influencer Management activities. It is important to clarify and establish consensus regarding the outcomes you expect to achieve, in qualitative terms, at least. For example, you might seek to increase marketing outcomes such as taking share away from a competitor, establishing a new market, or increasing engagement with content shared by your experts such as white paper downloads. Or you might seek to increase appearances of your brand's experts at industry conferences.

In addition, you'll want to establish a consensus on expected relationships between influencer activities and business goals. For example, if you want your experts to support downloads of your white papers, clarify how you expect them to do it. Further, it is critical that you prioritize employee mobilization according to the objectives and the employee expertise required to support social strategies.

Then, clarify the business units and functional teams that your experts will support. For example, will they work with marketing, sales, customer service, recruiting, or some mixture of those teams?

Finally, specify the most important milestones you expect to achieve in your Influencer Management program. For example, these could include the number of employees you want to equip and empower by the end of the year, the percent share you want to take from a competitor, or the number of white papers you want to have downloaded by traffic that comes from your influencers' blogs.

Influencer Inventory and Ecosystem

Once you establish consensus about your agenda for embarking on a social employee program, you then need to get the lay of the land—to understand who influences the online conversations that your brand cares about.

First, identify sector-specific or topic-specific influencers for inclusion in your program. Generic metrics such as total followers and proprietary influencer scores will not do the trick for the following reasons, which we describe in Chapter 5, You Will Measure New Things in New Ways:

- No tie to your business goals
- Vague links to your target audiences
- Inability to deliberately improve

Instead, you need to understand precisely who influences specific topics that impact your brand or your brand's goals.

The best approach involves research to determine who influences online conversations, and you should conduct that research through two means: First, ask employees or partners. They probably already know who most of the important influencers are or will begin to understand them as your program evolves. They may also be members of velvet rope communities that would be relevant to your goals. Second, consider purchasing a report or commission research from an established organization that conducts influencer analysis.

Do not rely on automated scores that are publicly available. Instead, you must work with a team or person who is skilled at understanding how you define the topics that you want to assess, as well as identifying the people who truly influence any particular topic, as defined by you.

When you begin this exercise, you need to establish a common definition of *influencer* among your team members. As Duncan Watts said:

> Everyone has their own definition of an "influencer" and they're rarely the same definition: sometimes the term is used to refer to "ordinary" individuals whose influence propagates via direct interpersonal networks. Other times it is used to refer to celebrities like Oprah Winfrey, whose influence propagates via the mass media. And at other times still it is used to refer to intermediate cases such as bloggers, columnists, experts, authors, and other semi-public figures whose influence is some mixture of mass and personal influence.[1]

After you identify influencers, prioritize those influencers for treatment. For example, you might wish to establish new relationships with some of the influencers, but you will likely not have the resources to pursue all of them at the same time. Or, you might find some of them more difficult to reach, due

1. Dubois, Lou. "Why Social Influence Matters to Businesses." 31 March 2011. http://bit.ly/InfluenceMatters.

to their relative fame or busy jobs or because they're members of velvet rope communities. So, you need to prioritize.

As Neil Beam, Director of Client Relations at MotiveQuest, says,

> You have to rank influencers differently, depending on your goals. If you're focused on customer service, you want to look for people who are knowledgeable about your products, constructive in their interactions, and have posted solutions of some type in the past.[2]

If your goals are more focused on selling, you need to understand the extent to which people in your target audience advocate for brands or products. For one consumer brand, the team at MotiveQuest found that 78 percent of people in social media who advocate for a brand do so only once per year. Three percent advocate twice per year, and only 3 percent advocate three or more times per year.[2] Those proportions may be different in your industry, and with your audience, so you need to understand how your audience advocates in your industry. Then, you need to ensure that your influencer program is structured accordingly.

You might also categorize the influencers according to where they live or work in the world. This is especially useful for inviting influencers to in-person events, such as conferences or product launches. It can also help to plan tactics that support relationship development in person, such as lunches, dinners, or events that your brand sponsors.

As you work through your prioritization, seek to understand the relationships between the influencers. The figure below shows two extreme types of influencer networks, and most lie somewhere in between, but understanding the two can help you determine how to target influencers for relationship development.

Examples of Relative Density in Influencer Networks

Figure 4.2 shows loose and tight influencer networks.

Loose Influencer Networks

In a loose network of influencers, you find pockets or clusters of influencers who exchange information or influence each other, but they are largely

---

2. Beam, Neil. Personal interview. 2 January 2013.

Loose

Tight

- Each influencer focuses on a niche subtopic or region
- Low likelihood that content from one influencer will be passed to other influencers
- Invest in relationships with each cluster

- Most of the people who influence the topic know each other
- Influencers tend to influence or borrow from each other
- Focus on establishing very strong ties with fewer leading influencers, to subsequently influence the entire network

Figure 4.2 *Types of influencer networks*

disconnected from other people who influence conversations about the topic. In this kind of influencer network, influencers only influence their direct followers. Members of the influencer network infrequently link to and follow one another. There is low likelihood that content, preferences, or intent from one influencer will be passed along by others. In general, only that influencer's audience will see the content.

Sometimes when you see an influencer graph like this, it indicates that you defined your topic too broadly, but sometimes it's simply the nature of the online conversation.

In a loose influencer network, you'll need to invest the time to establish online relationships with at least one member of each cluster. That means you'll have to work pretty hard, and you'll probably need to prioritize clusters, so you focus on the most important clusters first.

Tight Influencer Networks

In tight influencer networks, most of the influencers know each other. They share information, and even influence each other. Members of this kind of network frequently link to each other's sites, are active in online communities and social networks, share each other's tweets and follow one another in multiple venues. There is a higher probability that content produced or shared by one influencer will be passed along by others.

One important benefit of this kind of network is that you can establish weaker ties with more influencers and still achieve your business goals. On the other hand, one misstep with only one influencer may ruin your presence throughout the entire network.

As one example, this kind of influencer network is often present among people who blog about topics related to motherhood.

Relationship Inventory

After you identify the people who influence the online conversations that you care about, then you need to inventory the relationships that your brand already has with these influencers. This inventory should include formal and informal relationships held across your brand, including official relationships managed by your Public Relations or External Affairs teams, as well as relationships that exist between the influencers and your internal experts, marketers, business partners, or other stakeholders.

You should assess the strength, health, and potential leverage of existing relationships. By leverage, we mean you should understand where existing relationships can be accessed to support brand goals. Sometimes, people may have relationships that they are unwilling or unable to leverage for brand goals.

Then, identify past engagements with the influencers, and determine each influencer's predisposition toward the brand.

Think about the topics that each influencer writes about and their attitudes toward the topics that matter to your brand. For example, do they tend to write about product launches, or do they generally cover trends in a specific topic area? Are they typically neutral or positive toward your brand? Are they well-known naysayers or consistently negative about your brand?

Also understand the channels that each influencer prefers and how they have responded to past outreach efforts.

Based on the information above, determine where you intend to engage with the influencer and how you intend to treat him in general. Then, determine a suggested treatment plan for each influencer you intend to engage, either reactively or proactively.

As you think about how you will engage various influencers, consider Figure 4.3, which shows how you should vary your treatment of influencers according to their type and who is best positioned to engage.

As you create your inventory, you'll want to preserve it in living form, so that you can share it with your team and keep it updated as people within your brand grow and evolve relationships with the influencers, and as you add or remove influencers from your focus and your team responsibilities change.

Some organizations use Google Docs to track influencers, and some use Web-based tools akin to customer relationship management or sales force automation solutions. As shown in Figure 4.4, your choice will depend upon the number of people who need access to the information, the rate by which the information changes, and the total number of influencers you need to track.

Remember that relationships between your employees and external audiences or influencers are very personal. In most cases, employees' presence and activity in social media has a mix of motivations such as self-expression, being part of a community, getting peer recognition, connecting with thought leaders, and so on. All of these motivations are deeply personal.

Those personal motives are what fuel people's effort to perform and connect online, so you have to be careful about how you approach it. It is critical that individuals are respected for their personal preferences and limitations. Don't force actions on your employees, as you will likely be ignored and you will alienate employees, resulting in people simply choosing to not participate in the program. As you bring new people into the program, you should determine the activities that each person is comfortable doing and respect their input.

For example, some employees may have natural talent in communicating a broad strategy, whereas others may be more effective in discussing narrowly defined product areas.

Some employees may have a natural affinity and skill for creating valuable, interesting, and professional content, but they are just learning the importance of promoting and sharing it.

Influencer Type	How Your Brand Treats The Influencer	Outcome Desired From the Relationship	Business Functions Involved at the Brand
Advocate	• Empowered to represent the brand • Preferential access to information, people, assets • Consultative role • Private and small group-setting communication	• Word-of-mouth • Advocacy • Customer support • Early warnings • Crisis support	• Community Management • Marketing
Partner	• Preferential access to information, experts, assets • Cross-promotion and shared use of assets • Communication through established partner channels	• Act as a proxy • Word-of-mouth • Asset leveraging	• Business Partner Relations • Marketing
Customer	• Communication to inform, motivate, nurture, provide service, create WOM, prevent crises • Communication through dedicated channels, executed through functions	• Repeat purchase • Loyalty • Word-of-mouth	• Marketing • Customer Service • Community Management
Bystanders	• Communication to inform, motivate, move along the purchase journey, prevent crises • Targeted through campaigns; occasional interactions through social channels	• Product or service trial • Purchase • Word-of-mouth	• Marketing • Community Management
Influencer	• Preferential (sometimes exclusive) access to information, people, and assets • One-to-one communication • Assigned relationship owners; clear relationship planning	• Preferential coverage • Improved sentiment towards the brand • Adoption of brand messages or ideas • Word-of-mouth • Crisis support	• Public Relations/Public Affairs • Marketing

Figure 4.3 *Illustrative influencer treatment model summary*

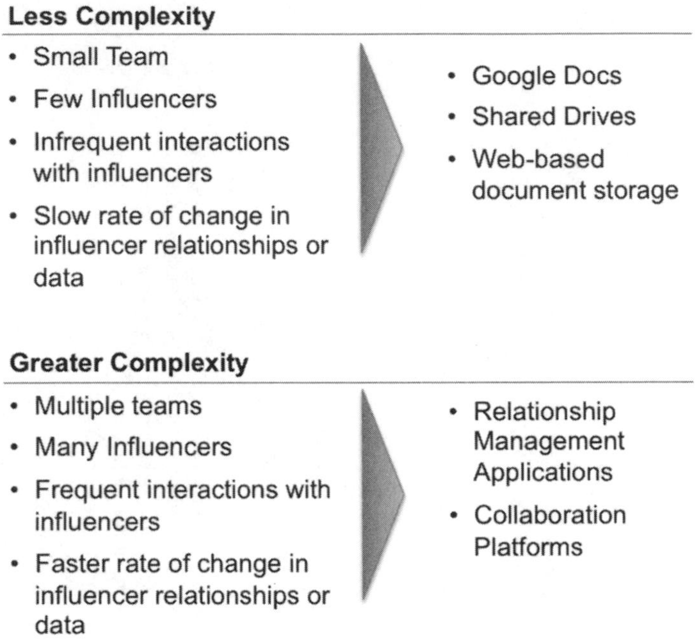

Less Complexity

- Small Team
- Few Influencers
- Infrequent interactions with influencers
- Slow rate of change in influencer relationships or data

- Google Docs
- Shared Drives
- Web-based document storage

Greater Complexity

- Multiple teams
- Many Influencers
- Frequent interactions with influencers
- Faster rate of change in influencer relationships or data

- Relationship Management Applications
- Collaboration Platforms

Figure 4.4 *Factors that determine tool selection for influencer relationship management*

Others may be more comfortable and skilled at promoting and distributing content that other people create. They might also find success in reaching out to influencers and followers to share that content.

You must seek to understand the preferences and natural abilities of the people you are empowering and help them to understand their abilities, as well. In general, they will be more likely to support your program goals with their most natural skills and preferences before learning new ones.

So, mobilize your team to support each other, and let those who are more comfortable communicating the broad strategy do so. Let those who revel in product details do so. And, in the process, let them mentor each other to advance the total skills of the team over time.

TABLET SMART SQUAD AT INTEL

In order to more broadly share the Intel tablet story, and to help consumers simplify their tablet purchase decisions, the Intel Ambassador team, led by Sabrina Stoffregen, joined forces with the Tablet Marketing team led by Sandra Lopez to energize a group of 250 passionate employees and their respective networks in social media.[3] Employees from twenty different business units with diverse backgrounds and a wide range of social media skills volunteered to join what Intel called the Tablet Smart Squad.

For each member of the Smart Squad, the Intel Ambassador team provided training, protocols, and access to an Intel tablet. Squad members published videos, tweets, status updates, photos, and answers to consumer questions on social media, technology Web sites, and retail Web sites. Because many of the squad members had access to an Intel tablet, some consumers received answers to their questions in video format.

In addition to engaging consumers, the Smart Squad also amplified retail partner promotions.

Instead of hiring an agency to create one set of content and hoping for it to go viral in a one-way broadcast of information, Intel unleashed the passion of its employees to create hundreds of pieces of content and conversations.

In less than four weeks, the team generated more than 1,800 social interactions, which amplified into 9,200 consumer interactions—an amplification of 500 percent. In one case, the squad drove so much demand that one retailer asked the squad to stop amplifying their promotion, which exceeded their expectations within 24 hours of activity.

In addition to dramatically impacting the business for Intel and its channel partners, employee enthusiasm exploded during the program. As one member of the Smart Squad said,

"The Smart Squad has been one of the most memorable experiences of my 15-year career at Intel. Not only did I have the opportunity to test-drive a state-of-the-art Intel-powered tablet, I had the chance to meet fellow employees across every geo and business group at Intel and forged new relationships and partnerships. . . Being able to show someone how our technology is connecting and enriching lives is a step up from just telling them the story. When I use my tablet around people, it takes the abstract concept of Intel technology they see in commercials and turns it into reality."

---

3. Personal interview. April 2013.

Conversation Analysis

In parallel with identifying relevant influencers, you should also seek to understand the nature and locations of conversations that the influencers join. In particular, identify the topics that attract online conversation in order to inform the ways that you approach influencers.

Then, determine each influencer's sentiment toward your brand and competitor offerings to help guide your approach to each influencer. For example, you would approach influencers differently if they mostly write negatively about a topic or about your brand when discussing certain topics. Also seek to understand your competitive standing in the conversation; that is, where your brand is being compared to competitors or competitor products and services. When your brand is compared to competitors, you should understand which competitors, on which topics, and by whom in the conversation.

Third, you'll want to understand the behaviors of your target audience and their perceptions of your brand, in the context of the topics you will try to join. For example, audiences may think that your brand is a great investment but a difficult place to work as an employee.

Finally, identify the channels and venues where relevant conversations occur. For example, consumer product brands often assume that they need to focus on Facebook and Twitter; however, many brands have discovered through conversation research that the majority of the conversations that affect their brand occur in other places, such as communities, blogs, or forums.

Take the time to determine the venues that are most often used by your audience and ensure that your team is engaged where it matters. Remember, this is not about just being social for the sake of being out there, in every social venue, it's about connecting and building relationships. So recognize the venues that are most relevant to your audience and prioritize your participation in those venues.

Although research is fundamental in driving a successful Influencer Management program, you must allow space for employees to experiment and develop their personal preferences. The fact that someone does not appear as an influencer within your research may not mean that your employees should ignore that person. First, your employees might identify and connect with up-and-coming influencers. Second, each employee will likely connect with people who see the employee as "someone like me," which will only benefit the brand.

Your strategy for developing relationships will be dramatically different, according to the venues where conversations occur. For example, when the majority of conversation occurs in Facebook, your brand page may be the core location for much of your brand's efforts to engage influencers.

On the other hand, audiences in communities, blogs, and forums often shun official brand efforts, especially when the goals of such efforts overtly benefit the brand. Instead, establishing relationships with influencers in communities, blogs, and forums requires a much longer-term and gradual strategy of establishing personal credibility by employees who are knowledgeable about the category discussed and give more than they seek to receive within the online community.

The amount of trust and influence any individual can earn varies considerably by topic. Specifically, the topic that you cover will impact the things you have to do to earn trust. In general, it is easier for a person to earn trust on a topic that is easily understood and where expertise is easily demonstrated.

For example, you can establish credibility in the art of quilting by publishing a series of self-produced videos wherein you demonstrate skills and knowledge of the topic. When you do so, most people will be able to understand your videos and, therefore, most people will be able to judge the level of expertise on the subject. On the other hand, if you want to demonstrate expertise in quantum physics, the videos are going to be more difficult to produce, and most people will not have the ability to determine whether you really know what you are talking about—but experts in this field will.

In addition, any person's trust and influence always varies according to the topic they are discussing. When the authors of this book talk about social media in business, people trust us as experts because we are practitioners and consultants sharing our expertise in the field where we've worked for many years. In addition, people can find a large history of content that we have published on the topic, and many online references to our work exist across the social Web.

However, if the authors were to discuss the topic of quilting, we would not have any of those assets, and it would be very difficult for us to establish our credibility, relationships with influencers, and, subsequently, our own ability to influence.

Therefore, you should empower your employees to establish their professional presence with enough consistency to establish authority on a topic. Both their presence and their style should be consistent over time.

Further, the content they develop (or you develop for them) must fit within the style of the person who publishes the content, their reputation, the channels in which they publish, their online relationships, and the audiences with whom they interact.

Tactics by Target Groups

Once you understand what you want to accomplish, the resources at your disposal, and their readiness to support your goals, you can begin to determine the tactics you will use to engage external influencers. You might begin by grouping the influencers and defining tactics for each group.

Also, the Word of Mouth Marketing Association publishes the Influencer Guidebook, which one of this book's authors, Susan Emerick, participated in developing. This guidebook will help you consider various influencer types and program considerations by type. This document is available on the Word of Mouth Marketing Association Web site at http://womma.org.

Capability Assessment

Once you determine the primary goals of your influencer relationship management efforts, you understand the people who influence the conversation, where the conversations occur, and how to interact with your audience, you will need to assess your existing capabilities.

In particular, you want to determine where you are ready to support the sustained effort required to build lasting influencer relationships and where you need to invest in additional resources, acquire new tools, or develop new skills with your team, including among your agencies or consultancies.

When you begin to plan your capability assessment, you'll want to cover all of the items in all of the phases of the Influencer Management framework shown in Figure 4.1. That means taking a look at each piece of the Prepare and Perform phases. Remember, influencer relationship management is a real commitment. It takes time. And it is a journey. You'll want to periodically take a step back, evaluate your performance throughout the framework, and continually look for ways to improve.

Operating Model

After you understand what you intend to achieve through influencer relationship management, and you've assessed your brand's existing capabilities, you will define what we call your Influencer Management operating model. The goal of this document is to help everyone understand how all teams will work together in the following four ways:

First, you will clarify the teams and individuals whom you will enable or support in the program. It is very important to ensure that you identify all of the people who will need to help make it a success and that you adequately estimate resources required to achieve the goals of the program.

Second, you will clarify the roles and responsibilities in the program and who owns each role and responsibility. For example, ensure that everyone understands who is responsible for identifying new influencers; who is responsible for prioritizing them; and who is responsible for tracking relationship-building efforts and who is responsible for engaging with them. In a small organization, one person may do all of those things. In a large organization, you might have small but distinct teams responsible for identifying, prioritizing, and tracking engagement with external influencers.

Third, you will clarify dependencies across teams. In most cases, when you launch an Influencer Management effort, you will find that your Public Relations, Communications, or External Affairs team already maintains relationships with some external influencers. You will need to decide how to manage those relationships. As another example, you might identify new influencers who are not engaged with your PR team, but your PR team may need to participate in the relationship when you initiate them. Specifically, your PR team may redefine their role away from owning relationships to brokering and coordinating relationships.

For example, if you decide that a prominent journalist is an influencer you want to establish communications with, then your PR team will most likely want to play a role in the relationship. And you need to decide ahead of time who will do what and when to ensure that everyone is able to work together efficiently and to avoid creating any miscommunication or duplication of efforts between the brand and the influencer.

Finally, after thinking through all of the above, you will determine where policies or guidelines should change to support program goals.

Measurement Plan

As you determine the tactics you will use, think about how you will measure success. Define a plan for measurement that includes the brand goals the program is intended to support, the tactics you will use, and the metrics you will track to evaluate success. (Also reference Chapter 5, You Will Measure New Things in New Ways.)

For example, set specific goal attainment targets from an established benchmark such as:

- Increase community engagement by your internal experts by 5 percent monthly.

- Increase the online share of voice created by external influencers by 17 percent, versus your current baseline, by the end of the fiscal quarter.

- Increase employee connectivity to influencers and their extended network by 10 percent, from the current baseline, within the next 6 months.

Before you commit to those metrics, you must determine how you will capture the data required to produce the metrics. Once you have the data, how will you analyze it, and who will analyze it? How will you present the data? Will you have a scorecard that someone produces manually and distributes by e-mail, or will you seek to produce a dynamic scorecard that displays on mobile devices, for more real-time understanding and decisions?

Presence and Content Optimization

Once you establish consensus on your business goals, you will need to take stock of your total online presence, including brand-owned and employee-owned accounts and properties. Then, you should determine the extent to which you must align those social accounts and Web properties with target audiences and communities. In some cases, you may need to create new accounts or communities and establish new resources to manage them. You may also find that you don't need some of the social accounts you have today.

Once you determine the set of accounts and properties you will need, you should plan for any changes to corporate properties and accounts. You will also need to craft a list of required and suggested changes for your employees. Then, you will work to optimize each of the accounts and properties for search engines and social media sharing.

When you begin your program, you will likely find a broad range of changes to suggest to your employees, as well as some needed in your brand-owned accounts. You may need to help some folks understand that, when they publish in social media, everything that they place online communicates. Their blog posts and tweets communicate, and so do their profile pictures, bio or "About Me" information, and the look and feel of their profile page or Web site. All of these things affect the level and nature of trust that they earn from their audience.

It is also important that your employees understand that placing information about themselves online can help them earn trust and credibility. As consumers have placed more of their information, needs, and wants into the public Internet, people expect to be able to find information about others online. In fact, placing information about oneself on the Internet has become a signal that one is trustworthy. While making oneself available to share expertise or knowledge does not confirm that one is trustworthy, the absence of such availability is a missed opportunity to build reputation online. While there are plenty of trustworthy people who do not place information online, they are missing the opportunity to provide a cue to external audiences and to earn trust and credibility.

Perform

The Perform stage is where you will execute your plans, measure progress, and continually refine your approach. This is where the rubber meets the road.

Relationship Management

Relationship management involves the continual tracking of your experts' relationships with external influencers. Much like in a CRM system, you'll want to maintain a list of goals, campaigns, interactions, results, and so on.

Typically, most of this tracking should be automated through a system designed for the purpose.

Content Management

Once you enable your employees in social media, one of the first things you will hear from them is that they need more content. Consistent content creation is very challenging, when combined with their regular jobs. Most of the people you enable in social media will not have professional design or writing skills, so there is an important opportunity for you to help them increase the quality of their content as well as the quantity, in many cases. In addition, you will want to provide them with images, videos, and other digital assets to help them support brand goals.

You're going to need a reliable process for defining and prioritizing their content needs, creating the content, storing it, distributing it to them, measuring performance of the content, and allocating content according to campaigns, themes, or other time frames when you may want them to start or stop using certain content.

In addition, you'll need a method for identifying when your employees create highly effective content on their own so that you can redistribute the content across your employees who can amplify the content.

Finally, content created by employees and brand-developed content are important to inventory and map across the customer decision journey so the material is indexed and easily available to employees or partners conducting outreach.

Overall, you'll want to strike a healthy balance between your editorial goals and the natural focus of each employee. After all, you are investing in their support for a reason, so you need to ensure that you have a process for ensuring you reach your communications goals, whether they be marketing, recruiting, customer service, or anything else.

Knowledge Management

A knowledge management tool is required to help your employees share information. In general, it serves as a central storage place for knowledge that helps social employees and partners find and build expertise, share best practices and lessons learned, and collaborate in their activities within the scope of this program. This kind of tool is very common in call centers, where people answer questions from customers all day and need a shared source of information and lessons.

Some organizations use Web-based sharing or collaboration tools such as IBM Connections, Microsoft SharePoint, Jive, or Salesforce.com. In a small business, you might use a shared storage drive, Google Docs, Dropbox, or Box.

Tools and Technology

Throughout the methodology described in this chapter, you will need to rely upon different tools and technologies. In large organizations, you may need to work with your technology organization to understand the tools available to you and to evaluate the breadth of vendors who can help you.

In smaller organizations, the tools may be different than those used by large organizations, but you still need to determine the right tool set to apply throughout the methodology. For example, a small organization might hire a small agency to conduct conversation analysis, whereas a large organization might hire their agency of record or a consultancy to perform the analysis as part of their retainer agreement.

In any case, it will be important to have someone on your team who is accountable for understanding the needs of your team and identifying the best tools and technologies to apply at each stage of the methodology. And remember, your needs will likely change as you empower more employees in social media and as your business matures in its use of social media.

Components Described in Other Chapters

Components described in other chapters include the following:

- **Lead:** These components are described in Chapter 7, How to Begin.
- **Measurement:** Program effectiveness requires a measurement framework tied to business objectives, so you will need to ensure that you establish such a measurement framework to determine the effectiveness of your program. See Chapter 5, You Will Measure New Things in New Ways, for a detailed measurement approach.
- **Recruiting, Training, and Coaching:** These components are described in Chapter 2, Help Your People Do Well.

Business Integration

The activities of your social employees should be coordinated with other official activities that touch external audiences. In particular, you will need to coordinate and integrate the activities listed previously with the following business activities, at the least:

- **Campaigns:** Coordinate activities and content from your employees with campaigns that you might run in marketing, customer service, recruiting, and so on.

- **Communities:** The primary difference between campaign management and community management is that campaigns usually have defined begin and end dates, whereas community management occurs continually; it's always on. Just like with campaign management, you should ensure that your activities and content used by your social employees is coordinated with activities and content used by your community managers. The two should work together and reinforce each other most of the time.

- **Affiliates:** If your brand uses affiliate marketing, you may find that some of your affiliates are influencers in targeted conversations. So, you will need to coordinate influencer outreach efforts to anyone who is also an affiliate. Further, influencer outreach activities should be defined to integrate with affiliate marketing efforts and content to maximize the extent to which they reinforce each other and to ensure coordinated timing of publishing in the market.

- **Search Engines:** Most brands that empower employees in social media hope to see positive impacts on their brand rankings in search engines. If that is one of your goals, you should ensure that keywords used for search engine optimization are also used by your employees engaged in social media and that employee-published content is optimized for search engines. Further, brands should provide guidance on how employees can claim authorship of their content in search engine results, for example, by using services like Google Authorship, which was launched in fall 2012.

Your Next Steps

1. Conduct research to determine top influencers who are active and aligned to your business imperatives.
2. Determine whether your program participants or extended team has existing relationships with these influencers; create a relationship inventory.
3. Determine segmentation for Influencer Management; prioritize who will cover which influencers.
4. Establish a community and feedback loop wherein program participants can provide one another with a regular update on Influencer Management and inform each other of new influencers identified through outreach efforts.
5. Conduct an assessment of current resources and capabilities, outline gaps, and determine a plan to close the gaps—for example, if you have not invested in conversation research to identify the people who influence the topics affecting your brand goals, define a plan to address that gap.
6. Estimate the number of connections your employees may have as a starting benchmark.

You Will Measure New Things in New Ways

"Not everything that can be counted counts."

— William Bruce Cameron

Empowering employees in social media requires clear and consistent measurement and feedback. This chapter shows you what to measure so that your program team and your social employees understand how they are doing and where they should focus their efforts to improve.

Most great revolutions in science are preceded by revolutions in our ability to measure or observe. For example, the telescope revolutionized astronomy, and the microscope revolutionized biology. In both cases, our understanding of our world evolved, and over time, we experienced more powerful outcomes.

In social media today, measurement technologies can help us to understand interactions between individuals and groups on a grand scale. But many people struggle to determine an effective approach for measuring and managing performance in social media.

In one survey, Forrester Research found that 49 percent of B2B marketers cited their ability to use analytics for decisions as their biggest weakness.[1] And it is a very important challenge to address. In fact, a McKinsey & Company study revealed that the effective use of data and analytics correlated with a 5- to 6-percent improvement in productivity and a slightly larger increase in profitability.[2]

We believe that people tend to struggle with measuring social media for the following three reasons:

- First, there is the data. Tons of it. So much data that we call it *big data*. Social data aggregators and monitoring tools give us filters to remove much of the data that is irrelevant to a particular need, but even those tools often produce far more information than a person can digest.

- Second, there are the tools. Even after all the acquisitions that occurred during 2011–2012, there are still hundreds of social media measurement tools on the market. None of them will address all of any organization's needs. In fact, many companies hire consultants to help choose the right bundle of measurement products, usually from multiple vendors.

- Third, people don't know what to measure. Social media are still very new to most people. In addition, the media and our ability to measure them are still rapidly evolving. And many people simply

1. Ernst, Jeff, David M. Cooperstein, and Matthew Dernoga. "Metrics That Matter for B2B Marketers: Revenue Impact Should Top the CMO's Management Dashboard." Forrester Research, Inc., 2010. http://bit.ly/ForresterRevenue.
2. "MIT's Erik Brynjolfsson on How 'Big Data' Yields Productivity and Profits." McKinsey & Company, August 2011. http://bit.ly/BigDataProfit. Video.

measure whatever metrics the social networks publicly display, such as Fans or Followers.

This chapter explains what you should measure when you enable your employees in social media.

How to Begin Measuring

At the most basic level, social media are all about relationships. Unfortunately, most measurement tools or approaches focus on *interactions* or *transactions.* Some tools focus on *conversations,* but that is still not the same as relationships.

For example, Facebook "Likes" are not relationships. Brands that define their goals based on a targeted number of Likes are not focusing on relationships because that kind of goal focuses on one specific interaction or transaction. Such goals do not guide an organization to nurture valuable and lasting relationships with customers.

In general, the most successful social empowerment programs provide fact-based, quantified performance feedback that encourages desired behaviors. The only way to do that is to establish a consistent measurement framework with clear metrics that everyone understands.

This section explains the clear and consistent framework we have developed over years of work with clients across various B2B and B2C industries, as follows:

- **Program readiness:** Continually appraise and assess the degree to which your internal capabilities are prepared to pursue and achieve the goals you set for your program or your team.

- **Employee performance:** Measure the performance of your employees in social media. For the purposes of this book, the term "employees" can include employees, partners, and affiliates. For all of those groups, measuring their performance is not the same as measuring their activity. Therefore, your measurement efforts should focus on outcomes that your employees achieve with their target audiences, not the amount of work each employee does or how much content they produce.

- **Business outcomes:** All of this effort should be guided by your business priorities: the outcomes that matter for your

Figure 5.1 *Social employee measurement framework*

organization. Maybe you want to find new customers. Maybe you want to hire the best people. Maybe you want to increase satisfaction among your existing customers. As you design your social empowerment program, you must specify the business outcomes you seek to support and then define a plan to measure the extent to which you actually help achieve those outcomes.

The three above areas are summarized in Figure 5.1, and the remainder of this chapter explains how to approach each of them.

Measuring Employee Performance

Fundamentally, your employees should build and nurture an online network of relationships that helps them to support one or more of your organization's goals. To reach that end, your employees will need to do three things:

- First, get people to agree to have conversations with the employee, or opt in to receive content from the employee. We call this *reach*.

- Second, get people to actually engage in conversations with the employee, consume content from the employee, or interact with content from the employee. We call this *engagement*.

- Finally, get people to share the employee's content or messages on behalf of the employee. We call this *advocacy*.

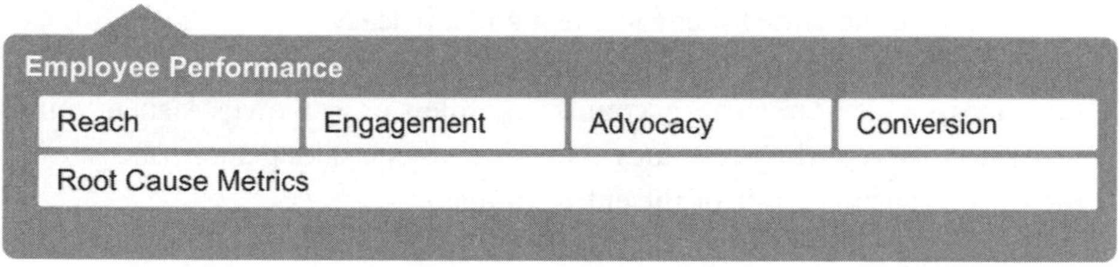

Figure 5.2 *Framework for measuring employee performance in social media*

It does not matter whether your employee is supporting Sales or Marketing or Recruiting or Customer Service. To be effective in social media, each employee will need to do all three of the things listed on the previous page.

So, you'll want to do two things for your employees:

- Measure how well each employee creates reach, engagement, and advocacy.

- Identify improvement opportunities through analyses of what we call *root cause metrics*.

Figure 5.2 summarizes the framework outlined here.

This sounds a lot like Marketing, and it is a lot like Marketing. That's because social media are all about communication and relationships, which are both core to Marketing.

In fact, many of the concepts that we discuss in this chapter apply to social media marketing in general—not just to social employees. Further, brands should measure their brand-owned social media with exactly the same metrics used to measure their employees. Reach is reach. Engagement is engagement. Advocacy is advocacy. It does not matter who owns the social account; the same framework applies.

You can measure one employee's reach in social media. You can measure the reach of a team of employees. You can take ten employees who work on one product and combine their reach with the reach of the brand-owned venues that support the product and calculate a total reach for the product to determine the performance of employees compared with branded social accounts.

You can roll that up across all of the products in a division and report reach at the division level. You can roll it all up to the corporate level and assess reach at the corporate level.

You can do the same for engagement and advocacy.

Then, you will be able to identify and leverage the most successful practices across all of your social accounts, regardless of who owns each account.

It's just like reporting revenues at the level of one sales person, one sales region, one business unit, or the entire company.

Reach

The number of people who agree to have conversations with your employees

Consider this analogy: In e-mail marketing, digital marketers always need to know the size and quality of their e-mail lists or their e-mail database. If you have a big list with a lot of high-quality leads or customers, that is a good thing. For the e-mail marketer, e-mail lists are a critical asset that must be nurtured over time.

Hopefully, each e-mail address represents a relationship that the brand has with a customer or a prospect who opted in to receive the brand's content.

Although it is true that a brand can buy lists of contacts, most marketers realize that is not an effective long-term marketing strategy and that it can be very costly. Instead, a high-quality e-mail-marketing list must be earned—one e-mail address at a time, with each person who gives you their e-mail address essentially agreeing to some level of a relationship with you.

Equivalently, when people follow you in social media, they establish a relationship with you. So, it is important to continually measure the size and strength of such relationships.

Therefore, the first important metric that we track is the reach of each social employee.

On Twitter, reach might count the employee's Followers. On Facebook, reach counts the employee's Friends, or a brand's Fans. Reach can be measured on every social venue.

Over the years, we learned that the term *reach* means different things to different organizations. For example, sometimes folks will say, "It's not reach that matters, it's *effective reach*." And they mean that it does not matter how many people receive an e-mail notification to download your white paper, what matters is how many people actually download it. And that's true.

However, in social media, we have to first attract an audience into ongoing relationships before we can then engage people within those relationships. Therefore, reach, as we define it, is a step along the path to the business outcomes that we care about.

Also, just like e-mail lists, all reach is not necessarily good reach. If you have an e-mail list of people who never read your e-mails, it does not matter how many people are on your list. Equivalently, if you have a lot of Followers who never read your content, or if you have different interests than the topics that your employees need to support, then their reach is irrelevant.

Therefore, you should periodically evaluate your employees' audience and work with your employees to help them build a targeted network around a shared topical interest, aligned with their expertise and your business priorities.

Your employees will improve their ability to help your organization only when they increase their reach among people who share an interest in targeted topics or conversations. In addition, your employees will create greater engagement with any given level of effort.

And that takes us to the second important metric for measuring your employees' performance: engagement.

Engagement

The number of times that people consume or interact with your employees'
content or messages

In social media, engagement means the same thing it historically meant to digital marketers: people consuming or interacting with content. For example, engagement could mean watching a YouTube video, or @mentioning an employee on Twitter, or commenting on your employee's post in a LinkedIn group. The critical thing to remember is that engagement counts the number of times people consume or interact with your employees' content.

To measure the social strength of the employee, measure the engagement with the employee's content. To measure the employee's contribution to your business, measure the engagement they create with the brand's content.

And do the same for the social media accounts that your brand owns directly.

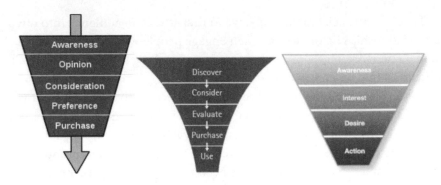

Figure 5.3 *Examples of traditional marketing funnels*

Advocacy

The number of times people distribute your content or message on your behalf

Digital marketers have been measuring reach and engagement for years. The new dynamic in social media is that your audience can tell other people about you or your content or your message. Your audience can *amplify* your messages or *advocate* on your behalf.

For example, people might retweet your tweet on Twitter, as an endorsement of your message, to their followers. Or, your audience might "like" your post on Facebook, thereby sending your post into their Facebook stream, where their followers can see your messages.[3]

Actions such as these amplify your message because more people hear it than otherwise would. When your audience shares your content on social media, they do your work for you. And this is one benefit of social media: greater reach and engagement with lower effort by the brand, which brings us to our third critical metric: advocacy.

For a little background on advocacy, we begin with a quick look at the traditional marketing funnel. Different brands use different structures for the marketing funnel; a few examples are shown in Figure 5.3.

In the beginning of social media, many folks thought that social media created a new step in the funnel: advocacy. Many people believed that the new, social marketing funnel looks something like Figure 5.4.

---

3. This dynamic on Facebook has gradually decreased over the years, as Facebook has slowly decreased the total content that any person sees from people in their network through a number of techniques.

Figure 5.4 *Traditional marketing funnel, with advocacy added*

But that's not quite right. In reality, people can advocate for a brand at any point in their experience with a brand or employee. Table 5.1 provides examples of target publics advocating for the brand, listed by stage of the traditional marketing funnel.

For an example of how customers can advocate throughout the marketing funnel, look at the online social KLM Trip Planner.[4] This tool lets people plan a trip with friends from Facebook from inside the Royal Dutch Airlines (KLM) Web site. It only takes one person to create a group and start the planning process.

People can join the group before they even decide to take the trip. And group members can invite others to join, even if they have never flown on KLM—thereby advocating for the KLM brand before purchase.

Or take the example of someone who reads a tweet from someone they follow, clicks a link in the tweet, and then lands on your company's Web site. Maybe they have never used your product, but they read about your offerings and they click a "share" button on your Web site as they proceed to consider a purchase. In that case, the customer advocates for your brand while still in the consideration stage.

---

4. KLM Trip Planner. http://tripplanner.klm.com/

Table 5.1   Examples of Advocacy, by Stage of the Marketing Funnel

Stage	Example Activity	Example of Advocacy
Reach or Awareness	Read a poster on a bus stop and learn about a new product	Scan the QR code on the poster and share it with my online network
Engagement	Download and read a white paper	Click a "Tweet This" button in the white paper to tell followers about the brand's thought leadership
	Comment on a blog post	Share a blog post with my network
Intent	Decide to fly to Las Vegas and attend a concert	Inform your network that you plan to fly to Las Vegas and attend a concert
Purchase	Purchase a book on Amazon.com	Click a button during the purchase process, and share the news of your purchase with others in your network
Loyalty	Purchase another book on Amazon.com	Write a favorable review about the product purchased, then share the review you posted with people in your network

At every stage of the customer experience, customers can talk about your brand within social media. As a result, you must nurture relationships in social media throughout the customer experience. You must be able to reach your target publics at each stage, you must get them engaged with your content at each stage, and you must motivate them to advocate on your behalf at each stage.

When you maintain ongoing relationships with your audience in this way, you establish relationships with what we call a *social core:* the people whom you reach, and who engage with you, and who would most likely advocate on your behalf (see Figure 5.5).

Ultimately, the social core becomes an asset of the brand, an asset that you should mobilize your employees to nurture and build over time.

The Social Core

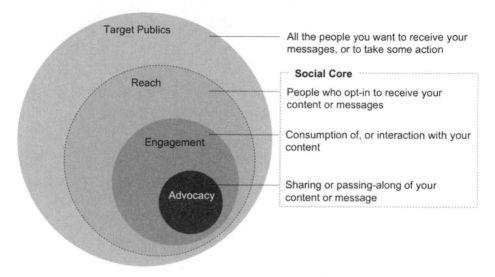

Figure 5.5 *The social core*

In addition, you should continually evaluate and measure the health and strength of your social core so that you can continually improve the degree to which you are making it stronger.

How do you measure the strength or health of your social core? Measure your brand's reach, engagement, and advocacy.

How do you measure the social core for each of your employees? Measure the reach, engagement, and advocacy that each employee creates.

Figure 5.6 summarizes example metrics for reach, engagement, and advocacy, the measures of the social core.

In the world of social media, audiences go away if you stop paying attention to them. They stop visiting your Facebook page or stop following you on Twitter. And then, when you try to run your next campaign, you have no audience to reach. Therefore, the most effective social media programs set

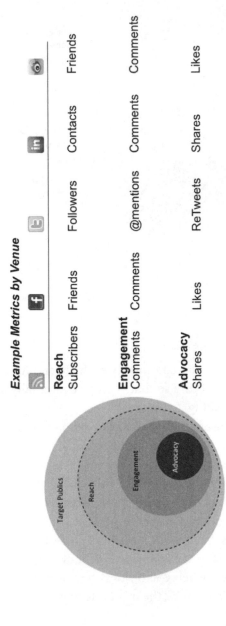

Figure 5.6 *Example metrics for the social core*

quantified targets for each of the above metrics and then assess the health and strength of the social core on a regular cadence.

In their joint research report published in 2012, comScore and Facebook[5] suggested the following:

> . . . brands should focus on benchmarking and optimizing on the following dimensions to deliver against their broader marketing objectives:
>
> **Fan Reach:** Exposure in the News Feed
> **Engagement:** Fans interacting with Brand Page marketing content
> **Advocacy:** Expanding reach by promoting content to Friends of Fans through both earned and paid means

While comScore and Facebook use slightly modified definitions that more precisely fit the Facebook venue, the idea of measuring and optimizing reach, engagement, and advocacy are now mainstream ideas in social media. comScore and Facebook further stated that:

> Most leading brands on Facebook achieve a monthly earned Amplification Ratio of between 0.5 and 2.0, meaning that they extend the reach of their earned media exposure of Fans to Friends of Fans by 50-200%.

When you enable and mobilize your employees to build trusted, ongoing relationships with your audience, you ensure that the audience will be there to amplify your message during marketing campaigns, or to answer another customer's question, or to tell potential job candidates about the open jobs that you are trying to fill. When that happens, you spend less money to achieve the same objective.

Root Cause Metrics

Root cause metrics let you understand why one employee achieves more than another. Such metrics help you and your employees to improve each employee's performance in social media.

For example, if one employee achieves greater engagement than another, you would dig into the root cause metrics to find out why and to determine specifically which actions the employee can take to improve their performance.

---

5. Lipsman, Andrew, Carmela Aquino, and Patrick Kemp. "The Power of Like 2: How Social Marketing Works." 12 June 2012. http://bit.ly/FacebookComscore.

The following paragraphs explain some examples of root cause metrics that we have used in the past. You might use only some of these, and you might also create new root cause metrics that are more useful to your team and your objectives.

Topics

Ask yourself the following questions.

- Which topics does the employee discuss?
- How well aligned are the employee's topics to a defined audience?
- Is the employee consistent in the topics they discuss?
- Does the employee mix too much—or too little—personal content with the professional content?

Content

Content includes all of the attributes of the content that an employee publishes, such as the following.

- **Vocabulary:** The words the employee uses are significant. You might want to understand the extent to which the employee talks about the brand versus talking about topics without mentioning the brand. You might also examine whether the employee uses words that other people in the conversation use. Sometimes employees use jargon that is more technical than people in the online conversation are using, and sometimes employees use words that have unique meaning inside of their organization. Both of these examples could make it more difficult for external audiences to engage with the employee because they do not understand his content. Or, audiences may find the content off-putting or even boring. Of course, you and your employees have to strike the right balance for each target audience. In addition, this is a fantastic opportunity to work together with your Search Engine Optimization (SEO) and Search Engine Marketing (SEM) teams, who probably invest significant effort into understanding the words that your target audiences use when looking for products and services in your category.

- **Media mix:** If your employees are publishing only text in their tweets and blog posts, you might be able to improve performance by publishing content that engages the audience in different ways. You'll want to run well-structured experiments and analyses to determine whether each employee's audience responds well to images, videos, or audio content. Then be sure to leverage what you learn by helping all of your employees create and publish the right mix of media types.

- **Venues:** Does the employee discuss topics in the venues where the relevant target audiences discuss the topics? For example, employees who discuss server virtualization on Facebook will find very little engagement with their content. But the same employee discussing the same topic on Twitter and LinkedIn is likely to find a very engaged audience. You will need to guide your employees with social intelligence to ensure they direct their efforts into the venues that are most often used by their intended audience.

Timing

Ask yourself the following questions.

- How often does the employee publish? Too often, or not enough?
- Does the employee publish when their audience tends to engage?
- Are you considering the full potential audience around the globe?

Network

Ask yourself the following questions.

- What types of people are in the employee's network?
- How well is their network aligned to the audiences that discuss the employee's targeted topics?
- Is their network active in social media in the ways that correlate with the business outcomes that the employee seeks to support?
- Are they connected to any influencers?
- Do they follow any influencers?

- To what extent do they engage with influencers?
- To what extent does the employee's network overlap with other employees in your organization?

Presence

Ask yourself the following questions.

- Where does the employee have a presence in social media? Where do they publish and consume social content?
- How well aligned is the employee presence versus the targeted topics and audiences for the brand?
- To what extent does the employee's presence work together with your brand presence and the presence of other employees in your organization?
- What factors does the employee use to determine where they should be present in social media?

Influence Metrics

When measuring your own people, freely available influence scores can be challenging to use effectively, for the following reasons.

- **No tie to your business goals:** Such influence measures are incapable of measuring the business outcomes that you care about most. For example, if you are a tactical marketer who cares most about conversions relevant to your brand, your most critical metrics come from your Web analytics. If you are a brand marketer who cares about sentiment or a PR professional who cares about favorability, your critical metrics come from your social media monitoring tool. In both cases, external influence vendors have no access to the metrics that matter most to you, and you are likely to find little correlation between your internal key performance indicators (KPIs) and those externally generated influence scores.
- **Vague links to your target audience:** External influence measurement vendors do not know who your target audience is. They might assume that everyone discussing a certain topic is one single

audience, but even that is crude. For example, if you are target-ing CIOs on the topic of cloud computing, it doesn't really matter how many followers someone has if their audience is composed of people who primarily work in cloud-computing startups.

- **Inability to deliberately improve:** You have no insight into the scoring algorithm, so you can't coach your people on how to im-prove their scores. If you measure employees on something that helps them to become better at something they care about, they will be more likely to accept the metrics and to work to improve their performance. If you measure employees on something that they do not fully understand or they feel unable to improve in a way that they understand, they will not be motivated to work on it, and they will be challenged to know what to do. So will you.

Many people have written about the use of such influence metrics. As Dr. Michael Wu, Principal Scientist of Analytics at Lithium, outlined in his 2012 article on *TechCrunch:*[6]

[I]nfluence vendors do not properly validate their algorithm for the following reasons:

No Data: They don't have an independent source of influence data. So they can only validate their algorithm by gut feelings and intuitions, which is often not good enough. . . .

Overgeneralization: They validate their algorithm base [sic] on a handful of known influencers and try to overgeneralize their algorithm to millions of users.

Invalid Circular Validation: They use reciprocity data, such as likes and retweets (which are decent proxies for one's digital influence), for valida-tion. But they also use these data in their algorithm. This is a common error in model validation, because this circular validation process doesn't give you any information about the accuracy of the algorithm. To properly vali-date any model, you must have an independent measure of the outcome, and that means you cannot use any of it in your model.

So should you trust your influence scores? Just ask your influence vendor how they validate their model.

6. Wu, Michael. "The Problem with Measuring Digital Influence." *TechCrunch.* 9 November 2012. http://bit.ly/MeasureProblem.

Instead of using the influence measures described above, you should define a scorecard with the metrics outlined in this chapter so that you can give your employees actionable feedback, with clear ties to your business goals and with straightforward suggestions on how they can improve their performance.

Debunking Sentiment as a Performance Metric

Lots of brands like to measure sentiment as the key indicator of their performance in social media. Some combine neutral posts with positive posts and call it *favorability*. Some do not.

For Communications professionals, brand reputation is typically the ultimate goal of everything they do. Ten years ago, Communications professionals measured their performance by counting press clippings—the number of articles that mentioned the brand or carried a story that the brand wanted target audiences to hear. That was called *earned media* because the brand had to earn the attention of journalists who wrote the articles, as opposed to *paid media*, where the brand can simply buy distribution of their messages in banner ads or television ads, for example.

But earned media and reputation are not the same thing. The fact that lots of journalists repeated your message does not necessarily mean that anyone believed the message or that you actually changed anyone's minds.

Then, when text analytics tool vendors aimed their products at the emerging space of social media, and they offered communicators the ability to measure the sentiment of their target public's conversations, communicators thought they finally had a metric that actually measured the thing they were trying to change: the reputation of the brand. After all, when people talk about a brand in social media, we can reasonably expect that what they say reflects their true feelings toward the brand—at least, on the topic being discussed, at that point in time.

There is just one big problem with using social media sentiment to measure brand reputation: In most cases, social media sentiment does not strongly correlate with customer satisfaction or net promoter scores.

To be clear, online sentiment does not equal customer satisfaction or brand reputation. If you are reporting favorability to your senior executives, you are probably misleading yourself and them. The paragraphs below explain how we know.

In 2009, Chris Boudreaux, one of this book's co-authors, partnered with Dr. Wendy Moe of the University of Maryland and Dr. David Schweidel of the University of Wisconsin to determine whether a brand could infer customer satisfaction from online conversations.

The team compared one year of monthly customer satisfaction surveys against social media posts from the same year. The surveys came from a technology brand based in the western United States, with operations and customers around the world. The brand distributed the surveys to its customers once a month. The social media records were randomly sampled from public online social venues such as Twitter, Facebook, blogs, and online forums. The social media records were then coded by hand for positive or negative sentiment toward the brand and its products. That is, the sentiment of each record was assessed by a person who read the record and then scored its sentiment toward the specified brand and products. That's about as accurate a sentiment scoring as you could ever get.

When the researchers looked at the relationship between the online sentiment scores and the customer satisfaction survey scores, they found a correlation near zero. Very discouraging.

However, the researchers then identified statistical biases in the data and were able to develop a model that achieved a 0.629 correlation between social media conversations and the customer satisfaction surveys.

The problem is that different venues experience different sentiment for different reasons. This causes raw sentiment scores to diverge from true brand reputation. For example, the share of negative brand mentions in an online forum tends to be greater than the share of negative online mentions on Twitter. Why? Because people go to forums to solve problems, so conversations in forums tend to have negative sentiment. But, as our research found, that does not necessarily mean that people in forums have lower sentiment toward the brand overall.

And that is just one reason why communicators who seek to measure their performance with online sentiment must develop a predictive model that translates online sentiment to the metric they really care about, which is usually customer satisfaction, brand awareness, or brand reputation. There are many other factors that bias raw sentiment and which must be incorporated into this kind of model. It can be done, but it takes some work by people who know how to build such models.

The important lesson for anyone measuring social media is that sentiment in online conversations probably does not reflect your customers' satisfaction with your brand. And movements in online sentiment probably do not reflect movements in customer satisfaction or true customer sentiment toward your brand. In fact, online sentiment may increase one month while scores from traditional satisfaction surveys decrease. In our research, we saw exactly that.

Instead of using sentiment to measure performance, we suggest using it in the following ways:

- Instead of reporting sentiment to your leadership, try reporting "complaints"—the things you need to change to improve your net promoter score, or customer satisfaction. Then measure the number of problems solved per month. Sentiment is not actionable, but complaints are.

- If you want to use online conversations to understand customer sentiment in more real-time, then you need to build a predictive model that translates online sentiment scores into the metrics that you care about, and it needs to be developed specifically for your industry. And you need to hire experienced people to do it.

- Use sentiment as a warning indicator to alert you to emerging topics in the conversation that might need your attention, such as an emerging communications crisis or a problem with your product.

- Use sentiment scores to identify nice things that people say about your brand, and then consider how you can engage in those conversations for the benefit of the brand.

But never assume that your brand has suffered just because online sentiment decreased in the most recent report. Also never assume that your brand is doing better just because online sentiment increased in the most recent report. It's simply unlikely to be true. Either way.

If you would like to read the details of the research, they are available online.[7]

---

7. Schweidel, David A., Wendy W. Moe, and Chris Boudreaux. "Listening in on Online Conversations: Measuring Brand Sentiment with Social Media." June 2011. http://bit.ly/Sentiment-Study.

Outcomes: Measuring Business Impact

When an organization invests in training and supporting employees to engage in social media on behalf of the brand, the organization always hopes to achieve some set of business outcomes. Examples can include the following:

- Increasing awareness of the brand
- Improving brand position in search engine results
- Making it easier for customers to find answers to their questions online
- Improving the brand's ability to hire the best job candidates

The excerpt from a brand scorecard shown in Figure 5.7 provides an even more detailed example.

Social media do not change the measures of business success. In fact, your investments in social media should be held accountable to the same business metrics that you used before social media. Conversions and purchases have not changed in their importance, for example. Keep measuring those.

Business Goal	Evidence	Expert Metric
Market Interest	Search Volumes for Branded Keywords	• Conversation volumes with SEO keywords
		• ReTweets of links to brand digital assets
Brand Awareness	Organic Search Rankings	• Mentions of brand experts in targeted conversations

Figure 5.7 *Brand scorecard excerpt: tying employee performance in social media to business goals*

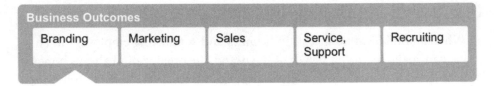

Figure 5.8 *Measurement framework for business outcomes*

The key is to define reasonable relationships between the efforts of your employees and the business outcomes you seek. Then try to measure the extent to which your employees achieve those business goals.

For example, marketers might measure the degree to which an employee's advocacy yields inbound links to the brand's digital assets. Or they might measure the traffic that an employee sends to Web pages that list job openings in the organization through the engagement and advocacy that the employee generates.

The chart in Figure 5.8 shows how one brand organized the efforts of its employees according to its business goals. This framework let the brand measure the performance of employees and give them feedback to continually improve their contribution to business goals, over time.

Measuring the Program

Empowering employees in social media is a significant program to undertake and to deliver. Your organization must invest time, money, and significant effort. Therefore, it will be important to ensure that you demonstrate progress. In addition, you must vigilantly watch for any sign that the program requires adjustments along the way. Simply stated, you need metrics and reports that tell you how your program is progressing. This section explains the metrics you should use to assess and optimize your program over its duration through four groups of metrics, as shown in Figure 5.9.

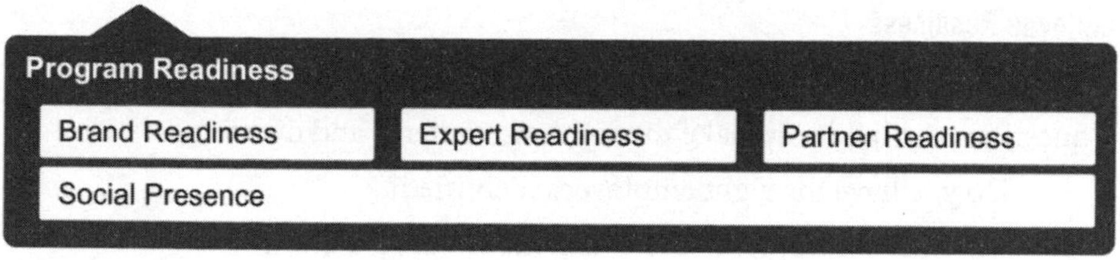

Figure 5.9 *Measurement framework for program readiness*

Readiness

Program readiness is the extent to which your overall program team is prepared to achieve the goals you will pursue. This includes everyone who will contribute to the effort. Not only your employees. For most brands, you need to think about measuring readiness in three areas:

- **Brand Readiness:** Are the people and processes within your organization ready?
- **Employee Readiness:** Are your employees identified, on board, trained, and equipped?
- **Partner Readiness:** Are your external partners ready to support your efforts?

Brand Readiness

When deciding whether your internal organization is prepared to move forward, the following questions can help:

- Do you have sponsorship and funding from executives who will be able to properly support the program?
- Do you have a plan for getting all of the needed people properly on board with your program?
- Do you have a plan for measuring the program and your employees?
- How will you reward employees and other program participants?

Employee Readiness

When deciding whether your employees are ready to launch, the following questions can help you make the right assessments and decisions:

- Do you have the right employees identified?
- Have the employees been recruited into the program?
- Are the employees' managers supportive?
- Are the employees trained?
- Have the employees been equipped with the tools they will need?
- Do the employees have an established degree of influence that you will establish goals to increase?
- Have you evaluated the reach of the each employee's network? What is the employee's connectivity to influencers?

Partner Readiness

Many brands use the following types of partners to help design, build, and operate their social empowerment program.

- **Agencies:** These can include your PR agency, which helps track and maintain relationships with some online influencers, typically journalists. You'll need to determine how they participate in influencer identification and relationship management.

  This can also include creative agencies, which may design or produce content that your employees will publish. You should determine how you will coordinate content development, improvement, and amplification between your creative agency and your employees.

- **Consultancies:** Consultancies are often used to help define the overall program, to plan the road map of internal capabilities required to operate the program, and maybe even to provide support activities. They may also help you build the business case, implement required technologies, and implement required business processes, such as content management and internal collaboration.

  More and more, agencies and consultancies both provide social media monitoring and performance measurement, so you

will need to determine who will actually produce your performance metrics and reports.

- **Channel partners:** You might consider including employees
from your channel partners in your social empowerment program. They may have additional relationships or resources that
help you achieve more than you would on your own.

In such cases, measuring their readiness is similar to measuring your own
brand readiness and employee readiness.

Social Presence

Social presence is measured at two levels, as shown in Figure 5.10.

Strategic Presence: Social Presence Inventory

First, you should have an inventory of all of the social accounts that your
brand uses and all of the accounts used by your employees. You'll want

Level of Optimization	Description	Example Attributes to Track or Optimize, for Each Social Account
Strategic **Social Presence Inventory**	*Inventory of all social accounts used by the brand and experts*	• Venues • People who own the accounts, and people who use them • Business unit or functional team that owns it • Audiences targeted • Languages used and regions covered • Products and topics covered • Influencer relationships
Tactical **Coverage Model**	*How each account will be used -- maybe for an event or campaign, or for ongoing influencer relationship development*	• Content to be used or published • Messages to support • Timing of engagement • Audiences to engage • Influencers to engage • Allocation of listening and engagement support resources

Figure 5.10 *Two levels of optimization for social presence*

to understand how each differs and how they relate to each other. For example:

1. Which languages do they use?
2. Which locations or global regions do they cover?
3. Which products, topics, or domains do they discuss?
4. Which venues do they use?
5. Who owns them, and what are the business goals for each account?
6. Who follows them, engages with them, and shares their content?

Having this list will help you to understand all of the accounts that you could potentially use in your program or to support brand goals. You should update this list at least every three months. Ideally, you should implement a process that lets your teammates add new accounts whenever they are created and remove them whenever the account is retired or when an employee leaves your company.

"For IBM this meant creating IBM.com/Voices, which is a dynamic list of feeds from official IBM channels and some of our best subject matter experts," said Ethan McCarty,[8] IBM's director of social strategy and programs. "Professional brand managers can add their channels to the aggregated view of IBM's social presence, if they meet defined criteria for quality and branding. Likewise, IBM technical and business experts can opt-in to be listed if their Twitter channel, blog or other feed is relevant to their work and delivers quality content and engagement."

According to a survey by Altimeter Group,[9] the average organization owned more than 180 social media accounts in 2012, so you may want to consider using a Web-based tool for tracking social accounts.

Then, you will need a way to ensure appropriate balance of presence across social venues. Each social venue should serve a different purpose in your portfolio, and they should all work together. For example, you might use Twitter to make people aware of new content that you publish on your blog, where you seek to engage the audience more deeply. Or, you might use Pinterest to drive awareness of your products and send traffic to a Facebook page where you can establish a closer relationship with them for the future.

---

8. McCarty, Ethan. Personal Interview. November 2012.
9. Owyang, Jeremiah. "Buyers Guide: A Strategy for Managing Social Media Proliferation." Altimeter Group, 6 January 2012. http://bit.ly/Proliferate.

As John Herrman of BuzzFeed said:[10]

> Twitter is where news breaks; Facebook is where news *goes*. . . . When
> a huge news story breaks, it gets swarmed by a self-appointed group . . .
> of Twitter editors which invariably becomes *the* source for new informa-
> tion. . . . [T]weets: They have value even without context, and come to feel
> like a *part* of the stories they accompany, not just links to them.
>
> In contrast, the modes of interaction of Facebook don't encourage story
> advancement, and carry a whiff of aggregation. The site . . . is great at
> building after-the-fact, heavily filtered digests; ...Facebook posts live in the
> context of each users' friend bubble. . . .
>
> Facebook referrals to this site, and to most, massively outnumber visi-
> tors from Twitter. Breaking news isn't hugely important to most people, and
> Facebook is for most people.

In general, the content that people publish in any venue evolves to fit the
venue. The 140-character limitations of Twitter let certain types of content
succeed and other types of content fail. The same is true for all social venues.

And this is not unique to social media. The same is also true for musical
venues. In particular, David Byrne of Talking Heads explains that musical
genres evolved throughout history to suit the venues that were prominent at
the time.[11] Essentially, the most popular venues create new styles of music
that best suit the venue. Stadiums created arena rock. Clubs like CBGB created punk rock. And grand halls like Carnegie Hall led musicians to create
an entirely different style of music. So it goes with social media venues. (For
more details of this phenomenon, see Chapter 1, Web of Trust: The Case for
the Social Work Force.)

In any case, your social media strategy and your social empowerment
strategy must honor the important differences and interdependencies between the various social venues that you and your employees will use.

The Paradox of More

Brands inhibit their performance in social media when they do too much. In
an analysis that the authors performed over a period of two years, we found

---

10. Herrman, John. "How Twitter Beat Facebook at Its Own Story." *Buzzfeed.* 29 May 2012. http://bit.ly/
    TwitterWon.
11. "David Byrne: How Architecture Helped Music Evolve." February 2010. http://bit.ly/DavidByrneTED.
    Video.

that, in every category, the brand with the greatest number of social properties nearly always had the lowest total reach in social media. The reasons are that (1) when a brand creates too many social accounts, it loses the network effects of social media, and its audience is disconnected; (2) internal resources are stretched thin and are unable to engage the audience effectively; and (3) when a brand publishes too much, people unsubscribe.

In addition, your organization need not strive to enable all of its employees in social media. Instead, you should focus on the right segments of your employees who possess the knowledge and expertise on topics of interest, aligned to the business priorities to the brand. Then, only enable enough employees to support the right level of conversations, with the right influencers and audiences, at the right time, on the right topics.

Tactical Presence: Coverage Model

Whenever you use any mixture of brand- and employee-owned accounts, you'll want to determine how best to use each account, as a portfolio. You should clearly define how each account will participate to ensure that you use all of them together in the best possible way.

For example, let's say our company is hosting a week-long conference. One approach that many brands take today would be to give all of your employees a list of URLs, images, videos, and messages and ask them to post the content in their personal social media during the conference. Then, ask them to retweet messages that are posted by brand accounts during the conference and to tweet quotes from your brand's speakers during the conference.

This approach has a number of problems. First, your audience has limited attention. There are limits to the amount of information they can consume on any given day. If you motivate your employees to all publish the same messages at the same time, you will overwhelm the audience. Your followers might perceive your effort as spam, as inauthentic, and as inconsiderate of their time.

Second, your employees will probably overtake the online conversation about the conference. Your audience may perceive this as rude and inconsiderate because no one else at the conference is able to have a conversation in the way they would like.

In the case of one global technology brand, the Twitter stream around one of its conferences was completely dominated by its employees. People who usually tweeted once in a while suddenly published 20 tweets in a day and shared the tweets automatically on Facebook. They were all quoting various speakers at the conference or pushing links to the brand's digital assets such as PDFs, infographics, and Web pages touting the brand's products and services. Audiences find these avalanches to be very annoying. This kind of behavior turns audiences off and makes them actively ignore anything that is broadcast about an event.

So, when you arm your employees to support a conference or any event or campaign, and you have a large number of employees active in social media, it is entirely possible to create too much buzz and to turn people off. You need to determine how you will avoid creating too much noise.

Clay Shirky argues that information overload is not the problem; *filter failure* is.[12] As Shirky asserts, information overload is not new to the world. In reality, more information has been available than any human could consume, since before the printing press was invented. The problem now is that the filters we use in new digital channels do not effectively filter out unwanted information.

Rather than bemoaning the volume of information that fills our channels—a problem we will simply never solve—we must focus on improving our filters and ensuring that we design our communication to work effectively within the realities of existing filters.

In order to address the filter failure that Clay Shirky describes, some brands are finding ways to use their employees as the filters. For example, Accenture uses internal networks of subject matter employees to identify engagement opportunities—such as blogs or tweets by clients or key influencers—through their personal social media. The employees are given tools to quickly share the content across their internal network, collaborate on potential responses, and then publish well-crafted insights that leverage the expertise of their global teammates—all within the time frames required for real-time engagement in social media.

Specifically, you have to publish content according to your audiences' filters. Seek to deliver the right amount of information to the right people. Think carefully about what your brand and your employees publish, who does it, and how often.

---

12. Shirky, Clay. "It's Not Information Overload. It's Filter Failure." Web 2.0 Expo NY, September 2008. http://bit.ly/FilterFail. Video.

For example, when you prepare for an event, determine who will publish before, during, and after the event. Then, also evenly distribute your employees' efforts across a range of publishing types. For example, have some employees discuss topics from the event in real-time, as they occur. Then, assign different employees to create more curated content that your audience can consume after the event. Design it for people who attended the event, as well as people who could not attend.

As Constantin Basturea of Accenture, said, "At many conferences, nobody actually puts together useful resources that people can take the time to consume after the conference—something like a Storify page of the speaker's main speech themes, or a blog post with links to all the white papers, infographics, and resources that the speaker's company published around the topic."[13]

Summary

Figure 5.11 summarizes the categories of metrics you should consider when designing your social empowerment program. It also includes examples of metrics that companies have used in such programs in the past.

Your Next Steps

1. Identify the business outcomes that a social empowerment program should achieve for your brand.
2. Determine social data sources currently being mined and measured.
3. Determine current measurement and reporting approaches used and who is responsible for them.
4. Determine how employees and partners could contribute to the business outcomes in the first list item above.
5. Identify the most important venues where your employees and partners should participate in order to support business outcomes.

---

13. Basturea, Constantin. Personal interview. March 2013.

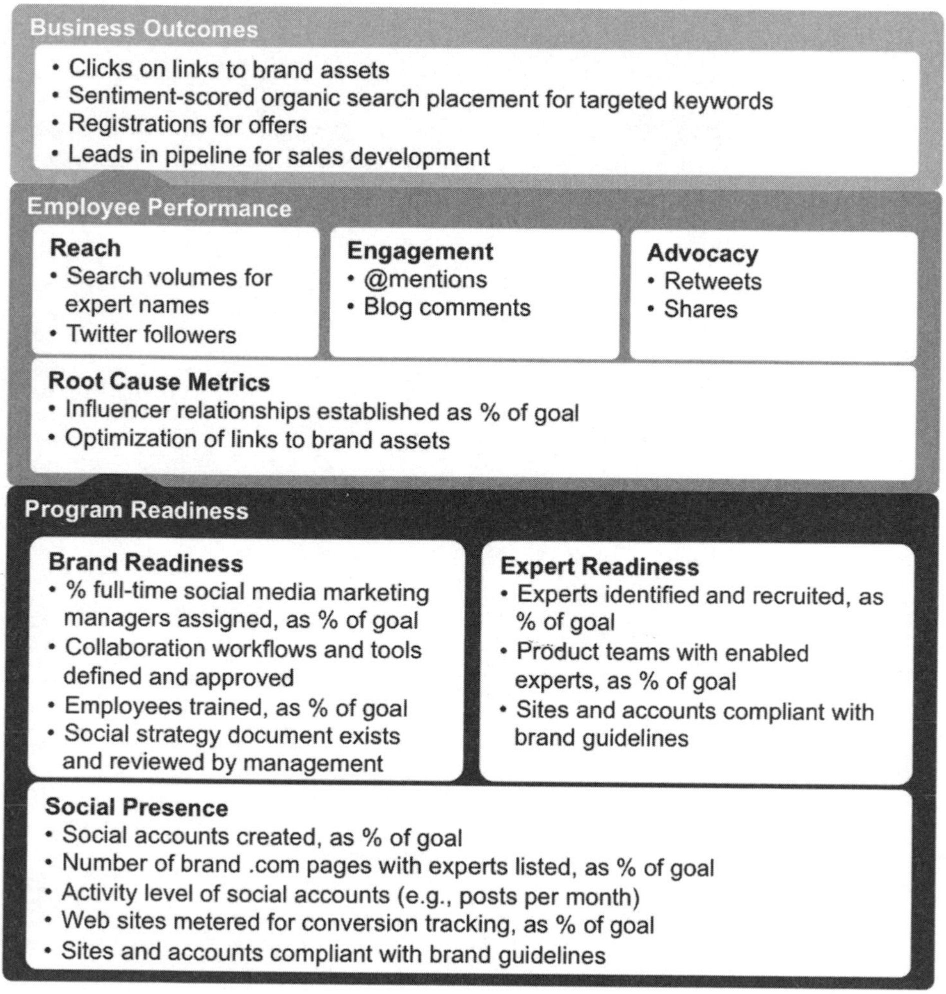

Business Outcomes
- Clicks on links to brand assets
- Sentiment-scored organic search placement for targeted keywords
- Registrations for offers
- Leads in pipeline for sales development

Employee Performance

Reach
- Search volumes for expert names
- Twitter followers

Engagement
- @mentions
- Blog comments

Advocacy
- Retweets
- Shares

Root Cause Metrics
- Influencer relationships established as % of goal
- Optimization of links to brand assets

Program Readiness

Brand Readiness
- % full-time social media marketing managers assigned, as % of goal
- Collaboration workflows and tools defined and approved
- Employees trained, as % of goal
- Social strategy document exists and reviewed by management

Expert Readiness
- Experts identified and recruited, as % of goal
- Product teams with enabled experts, as % of goal
- Sites and accounts compliant with brand guidelines

Social Presence
- Social accounts created, as % of goal
- Number of brand .com pages with experts listed, as % of goal
- Activity level of social accounts (e.g., posts per month)
- Web sites metered for conversion tracking, as % of goal
- Sites and accounts compliant with brand guidelines

Figure 5.11 *Example metrics from a social empowerment program scorecard at a global brand*

6. If your brand already empowers employees in social media, understand how the strength and performance of the program is measured, then assess the degree to which the program measurement quantifies whether the program achieves business outcomes.

6

Safety and Security

*"A lot of security problems occur because people think that, if they installed some technology, they are safe. But, really, they are just **safer,** and just for **now.**"*

— Gene Spafford

Empowering employees in social media is not risk free. Some of the risks are known, and some are new. In general, brands that empower their employees in social media must protect information and privacy, comply with disclosure requirements, and prevent competitive poaching.

This chapter describes each of these risks and provides tips for mitigating digital risks while pursuing business opportunities through socially empowered employees.

Protecting Information and Privacy

By the end of 2011, approximately 80 percent of the global online user population (over one billion people) was using social media,[1] providing a fresh
breeding ground for fraud and scams that were once successful on e-mail
and are now being revitalized to work in social media.

Public and private organizations are experiencing increasingly sophisticated cyber attacks, often due to cyber criminals taking advantage of
employee negligence. 2010 saw the largest number of security vulnerability
disclosures in history, up 27 percent, according to the IBM X-Force Research
and Development team.[2]

As stated by IBM security experts in a 2012 report on emerging trends
and risks in security:

> As individuals and organizations become parties to more connected, open,
> mobile and social forms of commerce, new approaches to exploitation are
> being devised. Not only are these attacks targeting information technology
> and infrastructure, but individual users as well, taking advantage of basic
> human nature. As a result, security can no longer be a discussion that re-
> mains within the domain of information technology professionals. Rather,
> protection in this new environment requires the understanding and vigilance
> of individuals at all levels of the organization.[2]

For the busy executive, security is not an issue that can simply be del-
egated; it must be embraced as another important component of doing
business in an increasingly complex and technology-driven world.

Organizations must appropriately mitigate the risks of enabling employees in social media. For employees who engage in social media on behalf of
your brand and have access to proprietary customer information, you need
to ensure that you do not place the employee or customers at risk.

There are at least four important risks to privacy and information security
that any social business should consider:

- False sense of security
- Abundant profile information

1. comScore. "It's a Social World: Social Networking Leads as Top Online Activity Globally, Accounting
   for 1 in Every 5 Online Minutes." 21 December 2011. Press release. http://bit.ly/SocialW.
2. Danahy, Jack, John Lainhart, and Eric Lesser. "Emerging Security Trends and Risks: Insights for the
   Business Executive. IBM Global Business Services Executive Report." Somers, NY: IBM, 2012.
   http://bit.ly/xforce-security.

- Differences between social platforms
- Insufficient technical protections

False Sense of Security

If someone came to you randomly on the street and asked you to break a $100 bill, you might consider the possibility that the bill could be counterfeit or that the person might try to rob you. On the other hand, if you were attending a party, you might be more trusting or more willing to make the exchange, even though you know no more about the person. The party simply makes the interaction feel safer.

Conversations in social media can often feel as though we are having a conversation with a person or a friend, even though the entire world can overhear the conversation. In addition, social media often make us feel as though we can be more trusting of strangers than might be prudent in reality. Without a clear understanding of who is really on the other side of any online conversation, and awareness of the full breadth of people who could intercept or overhear the conversation, we may risk giving out too much information or sharing things that we should not expose or information that could be embarrassing at some time in the future.

For example, consider a typical conversation on Twitter, where you can have a conversation that feels very casual, and maybe the person on the other end of the conversation asks for your e-mail address. It might feel like you are simply exchanging e-mails with one person, but unless you are exchanging *direct messages*,[3] the entire exchange is available to anyone on the Internet. While the interaction may feel informal and safe, and it may appear to have limited scope, these kinds of conversations can actually create significant risk of exposure because they are publicly visible and you may not really know who is on the other side.

In addition, conversations in social media are usually archived by the social media vendor, so the information you post becomes part of a permanent record to which many people have access.

---

3. "A direct message (DM) is a private message sent via Twitter to one of your followers. You can only send a direct message to a user who is following you; you can only receive direct messages from users you follow." (https://twitter.com. 26 November 2012.)

RALLYING THE STAFF
IN PEDIATRIC HEALTH CARE

For a variety of reasons, most medical practices shy away from social media. Patient information must be protected, and medical professionals typically work within a very busy schedule that keeps them focused on patients. They simply have no time for monitoring social media or writing and publishing content. In that highly regulated and very busy setting, the team at Kids Plus Pediatrics found a way to engage the full breadth of their staff in social media, on behalf of the practice, with tremendous success for their patients and their business.

Chad Hermann leads social media activities for Kids Plus. He explains that they use a blend of engagement on Facebook, Twitter, and YouTube to reach parents and child patients in their practice. Within their social channels, Chad ensures consistent voice of the brand, but he sources content from everyone in the practice. Staff members in various roles across the practice send him content that he can share with their audiences, such as links to content on other Web sites.

In addition, each physician takes a turn writing a weekly note to their patient and parent community, sharing an anecdote and providing helpful information. This approach lets each physician publish under their own name and establish their own presence in social media, while maintaining a reasonable burden for content development.

Kids Plus has been so successful at establishing relationships and credibility in its social presence that parents actually request to have photos of their children added to the practice Facebook page.

In most cases, medical professionals shy away from social media because of two fears: First, they worry about compliance with HIPAA regulations that require medical practices to keep patient information confidential. Second, they worry that patients will publish negative reviews of the practice online, for all the world to see.

At Kids Plus, the practice never publishes patient information in social media, and all children's photos are posted only with express consent of the parents. And in the three years that the practice has been active in social media, they have received only a handful of negative comments from patients—which provided them the opportunity to address issues directly—while receiving hundreds of positive and passionate endorsements from the patients who love the staff and the wonderful work they do for their children.

Abundant Profile Information

Employees who maintain an online profile and share in social media may give away information that can be used for a kind of attack known as *social engineering*. Sarah Granger of the global software security company Symantec described *social engineering* as "a hacker's clever manipulation of the natural human tendency to trust. The hacker's goal is to obtain information that will allow him/her to gain unauthorized access to a valued system and the information that resides on that system."[4]

To understand how social engineering works, consider the following fictional but realistic scenario:

1. In this example, the intruder targets a brand and begins by focusing on an employee to trick her into downloading malicious software. The intruder studies the employee's profiles and activity on Facebook, LinkedIn, Twitter, and her blog. Through those activities, the intruder gathers information that helps him trick the employee.

2. As the intruder profiles the employee, he finds that the employee enjoys microbrewed beer and running with coworkers, and she recently was selected to participate in a new brand task force on social media. The intruder also discovers the name of the employee's manager.

3. The intruder sends an e-mail to the employee, pretending to be a fellow employee. In it he urges the employee to open an attachment, which contains the malicious software.

4. Once the employee opens the attachment, it places malicious software on the company's internal network, and the intruder is able to carry out his illegal mission.

Many people publish information in their profiles that is simply not necessary to publish. In addition, many people accept social media connections

---

4. Granger, Sarah. "Social Engineering Fundamentals, Part 1: Hacker Tactics." *Symantec Connect.* 18 December 2001; updated 3 November 2010. http://bit.ly/SocialEngineer.

with people whom they do not know, thereby increasing the amount of information that is available to strangers in social media.

Specifically, some social networks allow you to limit the amount of your profile information that is available to the public, but if you accept connections with people you don't actually know, that kind of protection is rendered useless. So, employees need to (1) only input profile information that is necessary and (2) only accept connections from people who are appropriate to have access to the employee's profile information. When you empower employees in social media, your training program should include content that helps employees understand these risks and how to manage them.

Finally, individuals who are associated with an organization targeted by hackers may find themselves interacting with compromised accounts within their social networks. For example, it is entirely possible that intruders might break into an account of one of your connections and seek information from you, posing as someone you know and trust.

Differences between Social Platforms

Each social platform carries a different set of risks with different costs of managing those risks. As a result, it can be a challenge to define standards and best practices that work across platforms—especially regarding the types of content that are acceptable, the types of profile information that are reasonable, and so on.

For example, some platforms such as LinkedIn and Twitter tend to emphasize text input. In networks such as Instagram and Pinterest, photos and images are the dominant forms of communication. Podcasts require audio and often video, while networks like SlideShare focus on documents often created in Microsoft PowerPoint and Apple Keynote. Monitoring all those types of content and defining standards for each can be a challenge.

Therefore, your policies will need to blend two types of guidance: guidelines that apply to all social venues, and guidelines that apply uniquely to the select venues that matter most to your organization.

Unfortunately, too many companies still do not publish or enforce sufficient social media policies. In fact, a September 2011 Ponemon Institute study indicated that only 35 percent of respondents had a written social media policy in place; and only 35 percent of that subset actively enforced the policy.[5]

Since 2008, Chris Boudreaux has maintained the world's largest repository of social media policies[6] at his Web site, SocialMediaGovernance.com. As of this writing, the online database contained more than 200 social media policies from companies around the world and across industries, governments, and non-profits.

Insufficient Technical Protections

Social media, where someone can send you attached files like a picture or link to a Web site, can provide another avenue to penetrate your defenses, and that avenue may not be well protected. Many organizations have e-mail or Web screening in place to prevent accidental downloads, but few products scan social media connections that might provide a pathway to internal systems.

Actions You Can Take to Protect Privacy and Information

In general, there are four security areas that you should consider as you embed social capabilities into your business.

1. **Security policy and framework:** Determine how you will integrate social media into business processes, and then document or articulate the expected behaviors within social media, as well as within your existing tools that will use social data. For example, determine which types of data can be shared and how you will authenticate participants.
2. **Security awareness training:** People need to receive continual updates regarding the behaviors that you expect of them and the new threats that emerge all the time. Individuals who are highly visible in social media are most at risk for directed attacks.

5. Ponemon Institute. "Global Survey on Social Media Risks: Survey of IT & IT Security Practitioners." September 2011. http://bit.ly/PonemonRisk.
6. Boudreaux, Chris. "Policy Database." Social Media Governance. 2009–2013. http://socialmediagovernance.com/policies/.

3. **Technical and manual security controls:** You will need to implement some technologies and processes to monitor activities, detect attacks, and govern behaviors.
4. **Legal and regulatory considerations:** Invest time with your Corporate Counsel, Risk, and Compliance teams to understand any impacts you should consider from using social media for your business.

Gene Spafford of The Center for Education and Research in Information Assurance and Security[7] is an expert in information security, known around the world for his expertise. In regard to security in social media, he states:

> Like anything else in a business environment, the controls you put in place really should reduce risk. You can't make the risks go away completely, but if you can identify the important functions in your organization, and identify the risks of carrying them out, that's what we do for any kind of business.
>
> It's way too expensive and way too cumbersome to make a system that cannot possibly be broken into, and if you do, it will be so difficult to use that no one will use it.[8]

As stated by IBM security experts,

> Unfortunately, there is no software or suite of end-point security products that can be easily deployed to defend against the many types and approaches to social engineering. As with most threats aimed at human beings, the best way to manage such risks is through policy and education.[2]

Ultimately, no technology can prevent employees from publishing information they shouldn't. Instead, most organizations find that the key to preventing employees from making mistakes that harm the company is a thoughtful blend of (1) policies and (2) awareness processes that ensure that the employees understand the policies.

In general, policies should describe those classes of activities or tasks that employees are prohibited from doing with respect to certain types of data.

For example, according to Staff Sergeant Dale Sweetnam of the Online and Social Media Division in the Office of the Chief of Public Affairs of the U.S. Army,[9] the Army maintains a well-organized training program for

---

7. The Center for Education and Research in Information Assurance and Security. www.cerias.purdue.edu.
8. Spafford, Gene. Personal interview. 16 November 2012.
9. Sweetnam, Daniel. Personal interview by Tina McCorkindale, Associate Professor, Appalachian State University, 2012.

employees, soldiers, and their families that features *social media roundups,* distributed twice a month to public affairs practitioners and social media managers to educate them about social media topics. The roundups address topics such as privacy changes on Google, measuring social media, and managing a program with limited personnel.

In addition, the Army encourages family members to participate in social media, especially Facebook, even though this may pose a challenge if they post information about the soldiers, such as their location. Therefore, the Army relies on company commanders to provide guidance to their people, and the Army also provides social media roundups for soldiers, spouses, and their children to help them understand what information should not be included in their social media postings due to privacy and safety concerns.[7]

This is nothing new to most IT teams, but it may require some effort to determine whether your policies that affect employees' use of social media are complete, are correct, and align with the intent of your organization.

According to Professor Spafford,[8] you can begin by understanding the scope of what you are protecting, including reputation and privacy. Then understand the risks to what you are protecting, the capabilities of your platforms, and the business purposes of the social platforms your teams use.

And that's where a lot of things blur: business purposes. Employees have a blurred definition of business purposes, and the brand may also have a blurry definition so, for example, you may end up with people hosting personal Web sites on company hardware because there isn't a clear delineation.

SECURITY SUGGESTIONS FROM IBM SECURITY

In their 2012 analysis of security trends and risks,[2] the security experts at IBM published the following suggestions for employees participating in social media:

- **Enable security and privacy settings:** Understand the security and privacy controls in each social network, even if you are not an active user. To decrease exposure to spam, scams, and opportunistic attackers, set security and privacy controls to maximum levels.
- **Friend only friends:** Online con artists begin their attacks by attempting to build trust from their targets. Faking a work-related relationship via LinkedIn, for example, lends almost instant credibility for the attacker. Consider friendship requests carefully, and accept requests

only when based on prior real-world relationships or provable connections. Also understand that, if you accept a connection, people in your network may assume that person to be trustworthy.

- **Use caution with links and downloads:** Links and downloads have been a favorite vehicle for attackers to deliver malware via e-mail since the late 1990s. Carefully consider the source and appropriateness or relevance before clicking a link or downloading anything (particularly executable files, which end with ".exe"). People in your network may have been attacked, so be careful about content that comes from a third party.
- **Be wary of contests, gifts, prizes, and special offers:** Prizes and other special offer scams also date back to the early days of e-mail and perform strongly in social media. Scammers typically use this type of offer to direct you to a dead-end Web site that loads cookies or spyware to your computer. More often, they lead to fake Web sites that mimic legitimate businesses or brands. Either way, the scammer is collecting personal information from its targets.
- **Remain cautious about disclosing work-related information:** Consult the employer's *appropriate use* policies for social media when communicating information about the organization, colleagues, clients, products, services, and projects.

With appropriate policies in place, you'll need to ensure that you have adequate awareness processes in place. Some of the things to consider in your awareness program could include the following.

- How do you remind employees of the policies?
- How do you ensure that employees read the policies?
- Do you make employees take courses for certain policies?
- Should you tie consumption of the training to performance evaluations and rewards?

For example, IBM requires employees to take an online Secure Computing course, which covers ten essential practices for secure computing and includes a test for certification and completion.

As part of its global program to empower all employees in social media, with personal responsibility, IBM also published the following policies:

- Business Conduct Guidelines
- Social Computing Guidelines

- Secure Computing Guidelines
- Social Brand Engagement Guidelines

Each of those policies are delivered through the following initiatives[10]:

- Digital IBMer
- Expertise Location and Activation
- IBM Select Social Eminence Program
- Privacy Policies
- Enterprise Risk Management and Risk Assessments
- Social Recruiting Guidelines
- Social Selling
- Social Intelligence and Insights Practice
- Enterprise Social Business Management Council

Some companies prevent employees from being promoted or receiving bonuses if they fail to complete required training.

In any case, you will likely need involvement from Human Resources, IT, Legal, and other teams throughout your efforts around policies and awareness.

When you do begin to think about the technology component of your safety and security approach, Professor Spafford suggests that you might require employees to use different social media accounts for work and for personal use. In addition, the social media accounts that serve work purposes could be accessed only from company-approved hardware. As Professor Spafford says, "If you're on the job, and your job is to field requests through Twitter, you can do it, but you have to have a company-oriented account, running on a company machine, even if you're doing it from home."[8] Social media clients could potentially need to be running in a restricted virtual machine, without unfettered access to internal networks. However, that approach will not work in every environment or in every company.

Whether you segregate accounts and machines or not, you should clearly define the types of content that employees can download and the types of

---

10. Emerick, Susan, IBM Social Business Program Manager, Worldwide Digital Strategy and Development. 2012.

information they can send or include in their online profiles. Then, ensure that employees understand the reasons why.

For example, if employees respond to customer comments or questions in social media, there is really no reason for the employee to include their geographic location in their profile. Why? Because it doesn't matter where you are when you provide customer service and support, and that information could add vulnerabilities. It's unnecessary.

As another example, Chris Boudreaux worked with an organization that provided personal coaching services to college students with professional coaches working in call centers. The customer service model at that company was very unique because students would work with a single coach for an entire semester or year. This was a very different model than most contact centers, where customers likely speak with a different person every time they interact with the company.

In many cases, the coaches found Facebook to be the most effective way to contact and communicate with their students, who were essentially their clients. The students used Facebook nearly every day, and the coaches wanted to meet the students where they already were. In fact, many coaches found it impossible to convince students to interact through any other media, such as the phone.

But communicating with students through Facebook created potential risks to the coaches, who were, after all, employees. So the company created an internal policy for the use of social media by coaches. In addition to other provisions, the company first provided that each coach could use Facebook to communicate with students if they wanted to, but the company did not require it. Second, for coaches that found Facebook to be a useful tool in their relationships with students, the company required each coach to create a Facebook account that was separate from their personal Facebook account. Third, within those work-specific accounts, the company directed the coaches not to enter information in unnecessary fields that could create privacy risks for the coaches. For example, information about their home, their personal phone number, birth date, and so on.

Liz Bullock, Dell's Director of Social Media and Community, told us that the company's Social Media and Community University (SMaC U) training program helps employees understand how to navigate personal versus professional issues in social media through interactive role-playing and active discussion. Additionally, case studies and exercises teach judgment and critical skills to ensure that employees understand the risks to employees and the brand.[11]

In general, the brand has a responsibility to talk to employees, to ensure that they understand the risks, and to find the best tools for them to adequately manage the risks.

Periodic Reassessment

Finally, it is important for all brands to establish a process of periodic reassessment, or reevaluation, for all of the social media that employees use because everything keeps changing. The platforms change. Technology changes. Cultural norms change—in society and in your brand. You have to periodically revisit the guidance and tools that you give employees in social media.

As Gene Spafford[8] states:

Any policy you put in place now, or technology you deploy, has to be dynamic, because we don't know what the technology will be five years from now. That's where a lot of security problems occur; because people think that if they installed some technology, they are safe, but, really they are just **safer,** and just **for now.**

As an expert in researching these kinds of risks and their solutions, Professor Spafford has not seen a great deal of research that quantifies the risk, likely because this is still new territory for most companies and the security industry overall. In the U.S., at least, adoption of social media is still nascent. Social media does not yet provide a rich opportunity for people to attack it on a regular basis, and security breaches from social media are not widely tracked. As Professor Spafford states, "Statistics on computer abuse or these kinds of issues is very difficult."[8] Of course, this will change as more companies use social media.

As a result, most experts in this area are ultimately unable to determine the prevalence of these risks. Therefore, the solutions you pursue must depend on your organization, your organizational and industry culture, employment agreements you have in place, your technology infrastructure, and other factors. Ultimately, you will need to consult your Human Resources, Legal, and IT teams—in addition to others—to determine the best path for your organization.

---

11. Bullock, Liz. Personal interview. April 2013.

In addition to the preceding considerations, local privacy regulations are an important consideration. The full scope of relevant regulations and laws around the world could fill an entire book on their own, so we will not cover them here, and we suggest you contact your Legal team for advice regarding relevant regulations and laws in the jurisdictions that affect your business.

Complying with Disclosure Requirements

Over the past few years, jurisdictions around the world have made it clear that anyone who endorses a product or brand online should disclose their relationship with the product or brand, when a relationship exists. Disclosure requirements are not the same in all countries, but the general intent remains relatively consistent across jurisdictions.

Examples of government actions against brands who failed to provide adequate disclosures include the following.

1. The Federal Trade Commission settled an investigation of the social network aggregator Web site Spokeo for $800,000 for violations of both the Fair Credit Reporting Act and for lack of disclosure by employees.
2. Facebook settled a class action lawsuit for a lack of disclosure around its Sponsored Stories product by pledging to donate $10 million to charity and providing users more information about this ad product along with new opt-out options.
3. The Advertising Standards Authority (ASA) in the United Kingdom banned tweets published by Nike-sponsored athletes and required the athletes to delete the tweets (see more below in the section entitled, "Social Media Disclosures Must Be Obvious").

Social Media Disclosures Must Be Obvious

In June 2012, the ASA in the United Kingdom ruled against Nike and banned a campaign it was running leading up to the Olympics due to tweets from sponsored athletes about the brand because they lacked the required disclosures.

Government action began in early April of that year, when the Office of Fair Trading (OFT) publicly stated concerns with sponsored Olympic athlete

@WayneRooney
Wayne Rooney ✓

My resolution - to start the year as a champion, and finish it as a champion... #makeitcount gonike.me/makeitcount

1 Jan via Twitter for iPhone

Retweeted by LukeWhufcMarley and 100+ others

Figure 6.1 *Tweet endorsing Nike and banned by the U.K. advertising standards authority*
Source: Chernaik, Tom. "Case Study: UK Regulator Bans Nike Tweets for Lack of Social Media Disclosure." 2012. http://cmp.ly/nike-social-media-disclosure.

Tweets. Nike was one of the brands cited by the OFT because its campaign was shared in the personal Twitter accounts of two football (i.e., soccer in the United States) stars, Wayne Rooney (see Figure 6.1) and Jack Wilshere. Subsequent to the posts, the ASA received a complaint and investigated the matter.

As reported by Tom Chernaik, who is the Co-Chair of the Members Ethics Advisory Panel of the Word of Mouth Marketing Association and CEO of compliance software company CMP.LY:

> "Nike UK responded that both players were well known for being sponsored by the brand and argued that Twitter 'followers' would not be misled about the relationship it had with the players. The company further argued that the web address in the tweet was clearly branded as Nike, and that the message carried the company's known ad tagline—clearly indicating which tweets by the players were personal and which were ads."[12]

Although Nike indicated that the players were free, as part of the campaign, to independently reply or retweet consumer tweets at their own discretion, the ASA said it was understood from its investigation that the final

---

12. Chernaik, Tom. "Case Study: UK Regulator Bans Nike Tweets for Lack of Social Media Disclosure." 2012. http://cmp.ly/nike-social-media-disclosure.

content of the tweets was, ". . . agreed with the help of a member of the Nike marketing team."[13]

The ASA said the average Twitter user quickly scrolls through many tweets a day and that the marketing code states that ads must be "obviously identifiable." The ASA stated:

> We considered that the Nike reference was not prominent and could be missed. We considered there was nothing obvious in the tweets to indicate they were Nike marketing communications.[13]

It concluded that Nike breached the Committees of Advertising Practice code, so the campaign was banned and all of the related posts were to be removed.

Disclosures in social media are nothing new. Since the 2009 update from the U.S. Federal Trade Commission (FTC) that expanded the Guidelines for Testimonials and Endorsements, it has been clear that tweets, status updates, and other social messages require disclosure. More than the disclosure itself, the FTC requires that marketers:

- Mandate a policy that is in compliance with the law
- Make sure that those who work for them or on their behalf know what the rules are
- Monitor for compliance with their policies

CMP.LY HELPS BRANDS DISCLOSE

The FTC requires all material connections to be disclosed with a documented process. Disclosure information gives brands authenticity and transparency. Leading the way and making it possible for brands is CMP.LY, an NYC-based social media compliance and disclosure platform. CMP.LY provides coded URL's and badges that link back to unique disclosures.

Figure 6.2 shows a tweet that includes a disclosure link from CMP.LY for Jamba Juice's Ambassador Program, cited in a Mashable article in 2012.[14]

In the United Kingdom, both the OFT and the ASA stated that disclosures must be included in such messages, including when published by celebrities when they are paid or incentivized.

---

13. "ASA Adjudication on Nike (UK) Ltd." London: Advertising Standards Association, 20 June 2012. http://bit.ly/ASARule.

14. Oginsce, Michoel. "7 Tips to Enhance Influencer Marketing." 10 July 2012. http://mashable.com/2012/07/10/social-influencer-marketing/.

Figure 6.2 *Complaint disclosure enabled by CMP.LY*

Source: Ogince, Michoel. "7 Tips to Enhance Influencer Marketing." Mashable.com. 10 July 2012. http://mashable.com/2012/07/10/social-influencer-marketing/

The Word of Mouth Marketing Association publishes two documents to help brands manage disclosure in social media:

1. The "Social Media Marketing Disclosure Guide" at http://womma.org/ethics/disclosure/.
2. At the time of this writing, the Word of Mouth Marketing Association was preparing to publish a "Global Ethics Guidebook," for which one of this book's authors, Chris Boudreaux, participated in the development. When the document is published, it will be available on the Word of Mouth Marketing Association Web site at http://womma.org/ethics.

PROFILING POTENTIAL EMPLOYEES

The Dallas, Texas–based social media firm Social Media Delivered offers a service entitled Social Media Investigate, which is a social media background check that helps companies ensure that employees or potential hires would represent their organization appropriately online.

Eve Mayer Orsburn, CEO of Social Media Delivered, explains the new service, "Social Media Investigate fills in the missing pieces by reporting on someone's online presence and social media reputation. You invest time and money into finding the best people for your team, and our goal is to give you an unbiased report of their online activities to help you make informed decisions."

While this type of service may be useful to some brands, practices like this are illegal in some regions of the world, so global brands need to be very careful. Many brands decide to prohibit any activity that is illegal in any of the jurisdictions where they operate, even if such practices are not illegal in all of their operating jurisdictions.

In general, you should ask your Legal team before you use or define policies regarding services such as this.

FTC versus NLRB

In the United States, confusion sometimes exists regarding social media guidance from the FTC versus that of the National Labor Relations Board (NLRB). On one hand, the FTC requires brands to educate their employees on the fact that employees who endorse their employer or their employer's products must disclose their employment relationship alongside the disclosure. On the other hand, the NLRB does not allow employers to restrict free speech or employees' rights to organize.

In their attempt to comply with FTC Guides, some employers mistakenly prohibit activity that is protected by the NLRB. For example, some employers have written social media policies that require employees to disclose their employment in their online profile and to state that the opinions expressed by the employee are their own and not those of their employer. That requirement appears to be prohibited by the NLRB. Specifically, the NLRB provided that ". . . requiring employees to expressly state that their comments are their personal opinions and not those of the Employer every time that they post on social media would significantly burden the exercise of employees' Section 7 rights . . ."[15]

In addition, Section 7 of the National Labor Relations Act gives employees the right, among other things, "to engage in...concerted activities for the purposes of collective bargaining or other mutual aid or protection. . . ."[16] Historically, the Board has consistently directed that criticizing one's employer as part of a group effort to improve working conditions or in an effort to initiate group action is one of these protected "concerted activities." In the past few years, as social media have grown, the Board also directed that employees have the right to discuss the terms and conditions of their employment on social media sites.

In general, employers should require employees to disclose their employment only when employees make statements that would be construed to promote the employer or advertise on its behalf. If you require employees to disclose their employment in their social media profiles, you create two important risks to the brand. First, such a policy may be overly broad in the eyes of the NLRB or other governing bodies. In fact, when disclosure of employment is confined to that context, such policies have not been considered to be unlawfully broad. Second, if you force employees to state their employers in their profiles, the simple reality is that some people will interpret your employees' statements as reflective of the brand. For an example of how this kind of situation can get out of hand, see the case study below entitled, "Company E-mails Customer's Boss after He Complains about Them on Twitter."

COMPANY E-MAILS CUSTOMER'S BOSS AFTER HE COMPLAINS ABOUT THEM ON TWITTER

In December, 2012, Dan Grech had become frustrated about not receiving a gift subscription that his coworker ordered from iSubscribe UK. He emailed the company, but did not get sufficient response, so he tweeted, "Don't buy a magazine subscription through @iSubscribeUK. You won't receive it."[16]

Then, the exchange shown in Figure 6.3 ensued on Twitter.

---

15. Memorandum OM 12-31. Office of the General Counsel, Division of Operations Management, National Labor Relations Board. 24 January 2012. http://bit.ly/nlrbRule.

16. Long, Mary C. "Company Emails Customer's Boss after He Complains about Them on Twitter." *AllTwitter.* 10 December 2012. http://bit.ly/BossTweet.

Later that day, the Head of Operations at iSubscribe UK, Don Brown, contacted a Managing Director at Grech's employer regarding the tweets, saying, "We're trying to sort out [name] problem, but I do feel it is rather bad form for someone who is identifying themselves as being from your company to be posting such a sweeping generalisation about our company on a public forum like Twitter: https://twitter.com/dangrech/status/275560529618153472."

In his blog, Brown later apologized for contacting the employer. (http://bit.ly/FootMouth) and also stated, "One can't just say whatever one wants without being aware that this can have consequences; one's quick jibe can have real impact on real people. And if you say you're from a particular company, then your actions reflect on that company . . . "

In fact, it is possible to write a policy that complies with guidance from the FTC and the NLRB.

As stated by labor and employment attorney Alex Stevens of Haynes and Boon, LLP,

[O]stensibly minor distinctions or differences of degree in a social media policy can have unintended consequences, especially as the NLRB continues to refine its stance. For this reason, a social media policy should be drafted with an eye toward the policy's broader role in the workplace, as well as its interaction with the employer's other policies.[17]

Preventing Competitive Poaching

Competitors can threaten a social organization in three ways. First, competitors could try to poach your most visible and influential employees. Second, social media make it possible for your employees to publish data that you would not want your competitors to obtain. Third, competitors can undermine or take over your social media campaigns. For example, they might try to take over the conversation around your hashtag.

When it comes to protecting your people from competitive poaching, this risk is the same that you face with your best sales people and should be managed in similar ways. Your top sales talent personally own important customer relationships. They know your products extremely well. They know

---

17. Discussion thread on the blog post: Stevens, Alex. "Recent NLRB Social Media Report Raises New Questions." *Social Media Law Brief.* 16 February 2012. http://bit.ly/LawBrief.

Figure 6.3 *The Twitter exchange*

your weaknesses, and they know your strengths. There is always some risk that your competitors could try to steal your best sales people.

What do you do?

Some organizations write non-compete agreements that prohibit employees from selling for a competitor. Some organizations build their business and their customer relationships with assets that no individual employee can take when they leave. This is often the case at consultancies whose services rely on complex frameworks and technologies that an individual employee could never deliver on their own. Some organizations simply pay their best people a lot of money, send them on fun trips when they reach their goals, and, in general, simply take great care of the employees.

All of those options could be used to retain your most influential and visible employees, but each organization must choose the types of rewards that fit its culture and business model.

Loss of Data to Competitors

This risk varies by industry, so measures taken will vary by industry. For example, Zappos, an online shoe and apparel shop, has competitive concerns that differ from those of a management consultancy, whose services often depend on frameworks and digital assets that might be easily e-mailed to competitors. We discuss relevant issues and potential steps in the section above entitled, "Protecting Information and Privacy."

Your Next Steps

1. Determine which existing policies apply to employees in social media, including policies about security, privacy, and disclosures.
2. Identify procedures and processes required to ensure compliance with the policies that you find.
3. Start thinking about the extent to which your organizational culture will affect safe and secure employee engagement in social media.
4. Read the Word of Mouth Marketing Association guide on disclosures at http://womma.org/ethics/disclosure/ and Global Ethics Guidebook at http://womma.org/ethics.

7

How to Begin

"The only reason to give a speech is to change the world."

— John F. Kennedy

Empowering employees in social media requires broad support from across your organization. Achieving a broad base of support from executives and teams typically requires a gradual approach that first estimates the potential value of the effort, engaging executives for support and resources, then gradual deployment of the program in ways that let the organization learn and improve as the program scales. This chapter explains ways that you can build the needed support in the earliest stages of your program.

Once you believe that you can create significant value for your organization by empowering employees or partners in social media, the next most important priority is to get the right support from within your organization. You will need funding, staff, political support, and more.

In general, most program leaders have to build a business case, get some seed money to prove that the program works, then leverage early adopters who can participate in a pilot that proves that the concept works. Throughout those efforts, you must align your program goals to the social business maturity of your organization. The following sections explain how.

The Business Case

To establish an employee social empowerment program, you will probably need to build a business case to explain the value the program will create or the business outcomes that the program will deliver. After the program launches, you should track the outcomes from the program to ensure that it creates the value that you promised.

Building the Business Case

The business case for a large transformation program usually exists in two documents. First, you should develop a spreadsheet that estimates the costs and expected value from the program and a slide deck that explains the numbers for broader consumption and discussion.

A business case must include both costs and value. If you only estimate the expected value, you do not have a business case; you have a *value proposition*. It may be very helpful to begin by estimating only the *value proposition* to determine whether you should spend the effort to develop a complete business case. There is nothing wrong with that. Just be sure to develop the full business case, with costs clearly identified, before investing significant resources and energy into the program.

The most common sources of value from a social empowerment program usually include increased revenues and decreased costs, or efficiency and productivity gains. Revenues can increase when employees generate more leads or conversions. Costs can decrease if employees generate conversions at a lower cost per conversion—as IBM experienced and we describe in Chapter 1—or if employees answer customer questions in ways that cost the brand less per customer.

In your marketing campaigns, you may be able to create business value by empowering employees with the skills to condition the market, to persuade potential customers, or to create consideration and preference through their authentic trust and credibility with decision makers and those who influence them. In such cases, you may find that costs of leads, conversions, recruitment, and sales improve through your social empowerment program.

In general, the business case should clearly support the current goals of the business. Such business goals typically include goals for the current fiscal year or longer-term strategic goals. While you may be able to secure a small amount of pilot funding without having to show how your program supports the official goals of the organization, programs like this are only truly successful when they scale to touch the majority of the organization. In most organizations, that level of investment will only be granted if you can show how the program contributes to the most important goals of the organization for the upcoming fiscal periods.

Value Realization

After the program launches, you should establish a method for proving the program's value over time. This is necessary for two reasons: First, you need to establish a feedback loop to help you understand whether the program is on track. Second, you should hold yourself and your team accountable for delivering the results you forecast when you requested funding for your program.

As you develop the business case, think about the ways that you will track and prove progress of the program. For all of the ways you plan to impact costs or revenues, determine how you will track that impact over time. For example, if you believe that employees will be able to generate Web traffic that leads to conversions, determine how you will measure the traffic, the conversions, and the costs of the conversions. Also remember to measure the current state of conversions and their costs before starting the program, so you have a baseline metric against which to compare.

Value realization reporting should be a permanent part of your program management activities, so you will need to plan for resources who will gather, analyze, and report the necessary data. The number of resources will depend upon the scope of your program. Also, you should include some level of participation from your Accounting or Finance department because they will need to provide data and vet your analyses.

In our experience, most transformation programs decide not to include resources for value realization tracking, but we think this is a mistake. In fact, if you achieve your goals and prove your progress along the way, value realization tracking is the best way to secure more resources and expand your program.

Get Some Seed Money: Selling to Internal Stakeholders

Getting executive support is as much about educating the executives as it is about building the business case. They are not necessarily specialists in marketing strategy, or how to pull together a marketing program, or social networking. They will not have the time to stay abreast of the changes and emerging technologies that are occurring and how they've impacted the way people communicate. They may not fully appreciate how marketing, sales, and service must adapt to these changes to improve the customer experience. You have to be the expert who helps them know what they need to know, when they need to know it, so they can run the business. In this context, selling is more about consulting, educating, and enabling the executives.

In general, you should complete the following four steps to secure adequate support from executives in the organization.

1. Know what motivates the people who can get you resources.
2. Help them understand the shifts underway in the market and how this program will help the brand adapt with those shifts.
3. Find a champion.
4. Get a little money. Show a little progress.

Know What Motivates the People Who Can Get You Resources

In general, you need to know who is buying and what motivates them to buy. Then show how your program will help them achieve their goals. In particular, start by understanding the strategy of your business and the business goals for the current fiscal year. Then, build your business case for social media according to the ways that social media can support the business goals. Figure 7.1 illustrates various stakeholder roles across an organization and the metrics that they typically want to see in a business case.

Business Function	Metrics This Program Can Impact	How Social Employees Can Impact the Metrics
Marketing	• Cost per Lead	• Trusted expert employees generate greater referral traffic, leads, and conversions • Employees engaged in social media create links to your content, which boosts SEO • Customer satisfaction can increase when trusted employees are accessible and responsive
Brand/PR	• Share of Voice • Sentiment	• Increase share of voice by extending the reach of the brand • Develop more, stronger relationships with influencers • Protect the brand in times of crisis or criticism
Finance	• Costs	• Reduce spend on media • Decrease costs of content development and distribution
Sales	• Sales • Market Share	• Influence and relationships online drive sales • Employees engaged in social media impact consideration and preference, thereby conditioning the market into a favorable selling environment • Create new customer interactions • Enable affiliate, partner, and supplier interactions
IT	• Productivity • Efficiency	• Increase transparency that decreases time to find or distribute information, knowledge, and insights
HR	• Productivity • Talent Acquisition • Retention	• Leverage external talent through crowdsourcing • Decrease reliance on paid recruiters

Figure 7.1 *How social employee empowerment affects the metrics that business leaders care about*

Help Them Understand Market Shifts and How This Helps

In the above examples, you will often find yourself speaking with people who still view the digital world in terms that were defined ten or more years ago. You need to help them evolve their understanding to the realities of contemporary digital and social media.

For example, one of the biggest elements of your business case will likely involve forecasting the potential value from influencing online conversations—perhaps to increase awareness or preference for the brand.

Many business leaders today don't even know that you can measure online conversations in that way. You must help them understand.

Then, you must explain how your program equips employees to support the market shifts, which we describe in Chapter 1. Throughout these conversations, you should seek to understand how they see the world today and work to take them on the journey they may need to take. Demonstrate how your employees can engage target publics in ways that traditional communications cannot support. In short, use your imagination.

Find a Champion

Find a senior executive with broad trust in the organization who will use their network and influence to get other executives to support the program.

When you meet with them for the first time, explain the broad array of functional teams that are involved in this kind of program, then explain the benefits and risks to each of those areas of the company. Arm them for the conversations they will have with other executives by showing the benefits and risks. Seek their advice on how you can better portray the benefits and risks to other stakeholders.

Along the way, ask for support from the champion when you need it. Make it easy for them to help by specifying what you need, such as breaking down a roadblock, finding more time or resources, or making an additional investment.

Chapter 9, Manage the Journey, explains the role of the champion in more detail.

Get a Little Money, Show a Little Progress

Start by asking for just enough money to prove the concept works. Be clear about what you will deliver, and baseline or benchmark the metrics that you intend to impact, before you begin your pilot.

Increase confidence in your program by demonstrating progress in iterative sprints. Get some early wins. Regularly remind people of your efforts that succeeded and the impacts you achieved. Strive to deliver quantitative proof as much as possible.

Deliver insights and recommendations with each iteration. Show how you will adjust or streamline based on these insights. Be clear about actions you will take that will improve the program and yield even better results.

In addition to proving that you can achieve business outcomes, it is critical that you show the risks of not supporting the program. Some people are more motivated by risk avoidance.

Leverage Early Adopters

As mentioned in a previous chapter, in any internal social media program, you will encounter two types of people: early adopters and late adopters.

Early adopters are typically curious by nature and open to experimentation. They want to be the first to try something new. If the people around them are already doing it, they are less interested.

Typically, people who are early adopters of this program will be

- Already active in the social venues that matter to your brand. In the case of B2B technology brands, these venues are likely to include IT Forums, blogs, online communities, Twitter, and LinkedIn Groups.

- Active in offline activities where they share their knowledge and passion. Examples can include public speaking, local technology meetups, product user groups, or industry associations.

When you begin your program, plan to spend time identifying and engaging the people who will be early adopters of your program: the people who will feel excited to be the first to participate.

On the other hand, *late adopters* need to see people around them doing anything new before they will try it. When they first hear about your program, they will see it as simply an additional burden. The benefits will not outweigh the costs in their minds until they see people around them doing it. Once it becomes normal, or just something that everyone does, then they will want to do it.

In the beginning, do not waste your time on the late adopters. They will not be interested. In the worst case, they might develop a bad perception of the program because it was not mature enough for their standards. Get them involved as the program matures and they can see their peers deriving value from it.

Build a Pilot

Once you identify the attributes of people who are likely to be early adopters of the program, you need to pick one or two groups of early adopters to start the program, usually through a pilot. The best way to begin is by finding a team that has an open need for marketing in social media and that has budget to support your program.

Value can be demonstrated through measuring the difference between your existing campaign tactics and what you can achieve through socially empowered employees. Executives typically need to be educated on how people are the marketing power, rather than campaigns driven through media spend, so running a pilot helps to demonstrate how your people can drive clicks and conversions. Compare results of your program to typical campaigns, then use the data to develop your business case.

You will need a sales pitch for the early adopter whom you invite to join the pilot. You will also need a separate sales pitch for their managers and a third pitch to whoever is responsible to the area of the business where you will run your pilot; for example, a marketing campaign manager.

To help you structure your conversations with those three audiences, we list some of the key points to discuss with each audience.

Points to include when you pitch the program to an early adopter are as follows.

- Start with who you are and what you want. This may take more effort in larger organizations.
- Explain who is sponsoring the effort at the executive level. Demonstrate that the program is highly valued by your leadership, to the extent possible.
- Show the business drivers creating the need for this program. Include market, competitive, or customer issues and what might happen if the program is not implemented.
- Lay out a vision for the business after the program is implemented, and detail how it aligns with the business strategy.
- Outline the scope and objectives of the program.
- Show who is most impacted and who is least impacted.
- Explain what they will get for participating. Remember that early adopters are not looking for recognition as much as being

the first and getting access to things that other people do not get, such as:

- Content and digital assets that make it easier for them to build their personal presence in social media

- Support in connecting with or nurturing relationships with external influencers

- Recognition or placement on branded properties or social accounts, such as listing them on the brand Web site or linking to them from the brand blog

- Explain why you chose them. Your rationale should relate to the responsibilities of the role and why they are a fit. For example, when IBM selected expert employees to participate in their social media program for experts, many of the selected employees were already publishing works through white papers, technical journals, and so on. IBM encouraged this skill set but provided employees who have these skills an understanding of the value and opportunity for them to increase visibility of the content if they shared through social networks online.

- Outline the next steps for them to take and what they should anticipate from you.

- Give them the names of program contacts, a process for obtaining help or assistance, and ways to provide feedback.

- Share the schedule for the project.

Points to include when you pitch the program to the manager of an early adopter could include:

- Provide the name of the executive sponsor.

- Show how the program will help the manager and the team to better align their work with the imperatives in your business.

- Specify the amount of time that the employee will spend on program activities.

- Lay out the resources and support that you will provide to the employee.

Points to include when you pitch the program to a campaign manager could include:

- Explain who is sponsoring the program and how it aligns to business goals.
- Show the resources that will be at their disposal and how you can help them achieve their personal goals.
- Provide a timeline showing what you will be able to do and when. Do not over-promise.
- Specify what you will need from them and when you will need it.

Case Study: The IBM Select Social Eminence Program

As IBM looked into the future and saw the massive paradigm shift occurring in digital and social media, and the importance of people in the new, emerging paradigm, they realized that the most powerful way to maintain a leadership position would involve their greatest assets: IBMers. More specifically, IBMers recognized for their domain expertise who would actively participate wherever relevant conversations take place online. IBM believed that tremendous value could be created through enabling IBM experts and thought leaders to build their professional reputation, trust, and credibility among target audiences.

What they found is that the trusted experts who engage external audiences through their personal presence online tend to deliver brand information and messages to receptive audiences in the most effective and relevant ways possible. Specifically, each IBMer is often capable of creating calls to action that are more compelling to the audiences that they reach, compared with corporate generated messages. In addition, sincere, authentic messages from trusted experts have been found more likely to evoke a pro-IBM response from clients and prospects. Further, when IBMers participate in the online networks that are relevant to their expertise, IBM is able to gather invaluable feedback and market insights in the process.

To achieve all of this, IBM created the IBM Select Social Eminence Program, which offers training and tools specifically designed to help IBM business units develop and implement strategies that enable high-value IBMers to:

- Navigate the social landscape to identify targeted opportunities based on social intelligence
- Balance frequency and value of social interactions among target audiences
- Establish reputation, grow online influence, and foster relationships in relevant online communities
- Maximize value exchange of brand-building social interactions and communications

Using the program, IBM broadened its reach, deepened appreciation of the brand, and continued its ability to evolve and thrive in the digital age.

The Select Social Eminence Program helps experts and thought leaders to define a personalized road map for growth and success. In addition, it provides individualized guidance and support as each IBMer works to increase their visibility and influence among targeted online audiences.

Specifically designed as a customizable and repeatable model, the program provides tools and resources to:

1. Define marketing program objectives, strategies, and success metrics
2. Identify targeted opportunities, external market influencers, and venues for engagement, based on social intelligence
3. Enable and activate select internal experts and thought leaders to become highly influential participants, trusted collaborators, and respected voices in relevant online discussions and communities, by:
   a. Assessing current social engagement activities, behaviors, and preferences
   b. Developing customized action plans to optimize and fine-tune social skills and offering guidance on building relationships with known influencers participating in relevant communities, forums, and/or groups
   c. Curating content and digital assets to share in support of program goals
   d. Offering ongoing support and mentorship
   e. Monitoring progress against action plans

4. Measure the individual and collective impact of internal experts and thought leaders on marketing programs and company-wide *social business* goals
5. Increase consideration and preference for IBM products and solutions by increasing the reach, authority, and engagement of IBM employees

An early pilot of the IBM program proved that experts who build their network and sustain their engagement achieved three times greater conversion rates on traffic to brand assets versus those paid media tactics targeting the same objectives.

Your Next Steps

1. Identify the official goals for the upcoming fiscal year, and strategic goals for your organization, over the next 3 to 5 years.
2. List the leaders in your company whose business goals could benefit from increasing trust and advocacy with external audiences. It may help to consider the following questions:
    - How will the program help the brand capitalize on new markets or business models?
    - How will it help the brand get closer to your markets and customers?
    - How will it help the brand create value currently unknown, such as new products, services, or capabilities?
    - How is it that you can demonstrate value creation?
3. Gather evidence from other brands that have executed this type of program to determine how you will estimate the potential value for your brand.
4. Conduct social research and social network analysis to determine the opportunity for your brand in the marketplace.
5. Outline an initial structure for your business case, including the potential sources of value and the likely costs.
6. Sketch an executive briefing that explains the business case for your program and an approach you could take to pilot the program in your organization.

8

Build Your Team

"If you want to scale, you must teach others."

— Chris Boudreaux

This chapter describes the typical roles involved in planning, designing, implementing, and sustaining a social work force program. We explain the program management skills and roles required and perspectives on the trade-offs involved in using agency or consulting resources. Finally, we specify roles that are still emerging in this market and which you may need to create within your organization.

Because of the constant change that persists in social media, brands that em-brace social media embrace a journey. In addition to the dynamic environ-ment of social media, determining the right operating models for a brand requires flexibility and some degree of experimentation.

Social media have created important challenges for brands that are now required to understand, develop, and hire the skills required to implement and scale social capabilities across their organizations. All the while, new technologies enter the market, new methodologies emerge, and new skill re-quirements follow. For example, new jobs such as community manager and social strategist did not exist a few years ago.

Ultimately, brands must find the right balance of developing their existing employees and hiring new employees with needed skills or experience. The answer is not always obvious.

For example, in past years, many brands hired social strategists from other organizations, with the goal of quickly acquiring talent with needed social media skills. In many cases, the social strategists created significant value for their hiring organizations. But, in far too many cases, the social strategists floundered—often for two reasons: First, they were new to the organization; they had not spent the years required to develop strong internal political ties required to change the way an organization operates. Second, many of the social strategists did not have the change management and business opera-tions skills required to guide a change initiative.

As social media mature, the skills required to make social media work for business increasingly require traditional operating skills and industry knowledge.

In 2008 and 2009, there was an overwhelming number of people who described themselves as "social media guru" in their social media profiles. In 2013, it is virtually impossible to find anyone who leads social media initiatives within a brand and who refer to themselves as "guru." By now, most of the self-appointed gurus have realized that they need to bring more to the table.

In this chapter, we describe the team functions and roles required to de-liver the type of program we describe in this book. We begin by describing what we call program leadership roles, which are accountable for ensuring that appropriate strategies, business case, road map, funding plan, journey manage-ment, and program management are all in place. We then describe the program team, which executes the program. Finally, we briefly describe how your employees and partners—the program participants—fit into the program organization, and we discuss extended team roles, which typically include a wide diversity of skill sets, to help support the program on a part-time basis.

Program Leadership

Program leadership provides guidance, motivation, management, and resources to the program and typically includes a steering committee, the program leader, and a program manager.

Steering Committee

The steering committee is a policy-making body of senior executives that govern priorities across the organization. This cross-functional body of executives will ensure that the program has adequate funding, resources, and direction. They probably meet once per month to review progress, provide strategic direction, and ensure that resources are applied adequately. They may also help to break down organizational barriers.

This group's members decide the order of market programs that will be supported. In large organizations, they decide the order by which business units get enabled. The people who sit on this team typically represent each functional area of the business such as Human Resources (HR), Information Technology (IT), Legal, Finance, Marketing, and Sales. Many organizations include someone to represent their channel management organization, such as business partners, or local dealers in the case of automobile manufacturers.

Program Leader

A program leader is a senior executive who authorizes, motivates, and champions the overall program and performs the role of executive sponsor. This person has the ability to legitimize the program, simply through their visible endorsement and support. They either provide funding or work to secure funding from other executives. This individual has significant clout in the organization and is able to convince people to accept the disruptions that the program will cause.

A successful program leader sees the long-term vision and outcomes to be gained by enabling employees in social media. This person acts as a visionary and a motivator. The leader must make it clear that this program is a serious effort that will be seen through to the end. This person exudes enthusiasm and commitment, which gets others on board. This individual takes a leadership role to evangelize, gain support, and secure necessary commitments that result in the program being added to the agenda of other leaders in the organization.

Until an organization finds its program leader, we sometimes see organizations performing studies that go nowhere or people writing white papers that never become projects. If an effort does start before the leader is in place, it will probably fade unless an adequate program leader takes the reigns in time.

It is imperative that this person is viewed as highly competent and has a track record of leading successful programs. Nothing will kill his or her credibility more quickly than people seeing this person as incompetent or having a history of failed projects.

In most organizations, the program leader is not the CEO because CEOs tend to have more externally facing responsibilities, such as dealing with investors. Instead, this tends to be a more operational person—maybe the leader of a business unit or the head of Marketing. It should be someone who sees the value for the company overall, in addition to the potential value for his or her team.

Caretakers of the status quo need not apply for this position. This person must be ambitious, curious, resilient, and steadfast in their pursuit of the long-term vision. When these programs stall, it is usually due to inadequate commitment at the leadership level. People may blame lack of funding or regulatory concerns but, if the business case is properly defined and the program plan is adequately structured, funding should be available for at least a pilot.

Social technologies have evolved enough to support regulatory concerns in most industries. Regulatory excuses were very valid three years ago, but no longer.

Program Manager

The program manager holds daily accountability for the success of the program, including planning and execution. For companies that have implemented this kind of program, this person is usually an internal champion for the program and helps to sell the value of the program internally—maybe even convincing the program leader to support the program.

Responsibilities of the program manager typically include the following:

- Ensuring that the steering committee is engaged when needed and that they received periodic updates, which help them to support the program

- Ensuring the presence and use of a program work plan

- Ensuring that the program has appropriate resources and seeking help from the steering committee when resource additions or changes are needed

- Coordinating the different work streams, teams, or efforts within the program

- Identifying potential risks to the program and ensuring that the risks are mitigated appropriately

- Ensuring an adequate plan for change communications at all levels of the organization

While program management is a skill that most organizations develop, this type of program requires the program manager to have an appreciation for the skills and activities required to manage significant change in an organization. Ideally, the program manager will have led a large change program in the past. At the very least, this person must appreciate the importance of change management to the success of this program and ensure that someone on the team brings that experience into the program.

This person usually needs to be someone with strong relationships across the affected business units and functional teams—not someone from the outside. External hires tend to stumble as they learn the politics of the organization, internal processes for funding and governance, and other tacit keys to the success of this kind of change program.

Also, this person must inspire and motivate the program team. He or she needs to have credibility about his or her knowledge of the organization, in addition to knowledge of the solution and experience implementing this kind of solution in the past.

Program Team

The program team contains the people who design and implement the changes that become your social work force. They are the people who live in the business processes that are affected by the program such as marketing, selling, recruiting, or customer service. And they are the people who will operationalize the changes long after the program team disbands.

These people are a true, get-it-done team. They are not a committee. They are dedicated to designing and overseeing the deployment of the program. They are expected to embed the program into their daily work, not simply attend meetings and weigh in on decisions. If they do not do the hard work, no one will.

It is critical that the people who will live with the results are the people who craft the solution.

Typically, it is neither required nor possible that the program team work in one place. In fact, many successful program teams never gather in person.

Team members must be enthusiastic embracers of change. They must be open to working in an agile fashion to try and iterate around program elements at each stage of program development.

Typically, the program team includes participants from multiple business functions so that each member brings specialized skills aligned to the program categories. For example, technical, research, measurement, education, and training are all required skills within this type of program, and these generally reside in different parts of the organization.

Below are the most common roles included in the program team.

Social Empowerment Lead

This role defines the strategy and plans for engaging a target community through employees and business partners, then oversees execution of the strategy, including selection, onboarding, and ongoing optimization through measurement, training, and coaching, as illustrated in Figure 4.1.

The person in this role coordinates activities related to social channels, such as Facebook, LinkedIn, Sina Weibo, and so on. Typically, within a fully integrated program or campaign, the social empowerment lead works together with people who manage other channels, such as search engine optimization, online paid media, and television advertising. In those cases, the social empowerment lead is an expert in using social media to achieve organizational goals.

Within the programs they support, social empowerment leads provide guidance, training, and feedback to program participants (i.e., the employees and business partners enabled in social media). In addition, social empowerment leads coordinate the full lifecycle of social media efforts, including research, strategy, engagement, and measurement.

These leads participate in definition and creation of social experiences on behalf of the brand, and they mobilize social employees to help deliver the experiences. They also mobilize social employees to support functional specialists, such as product managers or recruiting managers.

They must understand the target community and, ideally, participate in the community directly. They also understand the business function that will engage in the community, such as sales, marketing, or customer support.

They develop coverage models that match employees to topics and external influencers, based on social network analysis. Then, they help to orchestrate engagement and relationship development among social employees, brand thought leaders, and their target constituencies.

Technical Development Lead

The technical development lead is the primary liaison to IT. This person ensures that the program gets the technology that it needs by creating functional requirements based on the needs of the program team, then helping to prioritize requirements and development efforts.

Education and Training Specialist

Employees will need to build new skills to support social networking and collaboration with decision makers, so you will need a training development specialist who can create an education and training curriculum. This person will lead the creation of training and help you maintain the training curriculum that will be required to achieve program goals.

Market Research Analyst

The market research analyst assists social strategists and community managers in their efforts to identify key external market influencers by conducting social network analysis and online conversation research. This specialist provides critical input into strategy and planning efforts through their supply of data and insights about the following topics:

- Influencer ecosystem
- Market share
- Market opportunity
- Changing market conditions
- Competitive landscape
- Brand reputation
- Conversation sentiment
- Conversation venues and topics
- Message resonance
- Organic search performance

Measurement Architect

You will need to design and implement a framework for measuring the performance of employees and social accounts to determine and continually improve the effectiveness of the program. The measurement architect oversees and implements the measurement framework, data collection, and data visualization. This person creates dashboards, a measurement plan, and a reporting schedule. He or she identifies data sources and analytics resources required to produce the dashboard or measurement outputs. In most cases, this person integrates efforts from multiple teams, including IT, which typically creates the solution; Marketing, which owns Web and campaign analytics; and whichever team owns social media monitoring.

Social media performance measurement will be new to most of the participants in this program, so the measurement architect will create a framework for educating program participants on the nature and appropriate uses of measurement data—including limitations on what can reliably be derived from the data. In addition, the measurement architect will coach social strategists and program leadership on what should be measured and how best to measure it.

See Chapter 5, You Will Measure New Things in New Ways, to understand the measurement framework we recommend.

Program Participants

Program participants are the employees who this program enables for outreach and relationship building in social media. As shown in Figure 2.3, your organization may choose to enable multiple tiers of employees in social media. Some will possess deep knowledge of and passion for your brand, and some will be a broad group of employees. Employees whom you enable in social media can include any level, business unit, or functional area of your organization, including HR, Sales, Marketing, partners, suppliers, managers, executives, professionals, Technical Support, and brand advocates.

In some cases, they may already demonstrate a measurable degree of online influence.

Their primary role will depend upon the business function they support. In Marketing, they might support marketing strategies by establishing their professional reputation, growing their influence, and maintaining collaborative relationships among target audiences.

They may volunteer, or you may recruit to join the program those whose domain expertise and experience complement program goals.

Extended Team

Most programs identify a set of people who only contribute to the program as needed, with no specified time commitment to the program. These people are the extended team.

They might provide internal process expertise, such as how to construct a business case, or they might help remove internal barriers to funding or resources.

While members of the extended team help the program only occasionally, it is critical that you identify and secure commitment from these people because they will be important allies to your program. They should be recognized in all program reviews and thanked for their contributions as appropriate.

This section lists some of the common roles and types of people who participate in extended teams.

Business Unit Leaders and Functional Leaders

Business unit leaders and functional leaders are the people who own the business goals that your program will support. They could be leaders in Sales, Marketing, Recruiting, Customer Service, and so on. They also include the business leaders who ultimately fund the social employee program.

The most important thing you need to do for these people is to understand their goals and their needs, then ensure that your program supports them. You have to get on their calendars, seek to understand their goals, and work with them to shape your social employee program so that it helps them achieve the goals of the organization. Only then will your program be truly successful for your business.

PR or Corporate Communications

Employees working on PR and Corporate Communications teams are usually responsible for all communications about the brand to external audiences. So, a social employee program needs to use their expertise, tap into their knowledge of external communications, and collaborate in planning and execution to ensure that the social employee program works together with PR and Corporate Communications efforts.

PR and Communications teams often define standards for communicating about the brand, which the social employee program must use. They may also have relationships with external influencers with whom your employees will interact, so you may need to coordinate influencer outreach with PR and Corporate Communications.

The paragraphs above describe how PR and Communications staff maintain their traditional responsibilities in the age of social media, but there are also important ways that PR and Communications teams must adapt their role in the organization to support a more social organization.

According to the Arthur W. Page Society,[1] Corporate Communications teams' primary responsibility must be to ensure that the company *looks like, sounds like, and performs like its stated character.* The Page Society goes on to say that achieving that goal requires professional communicators to adapt their operating models in two important ways: First, communicators must seek to engage individuals, in addition to audiences, publics, or segments. Second, communicators must spur individuals to action: to advocate. This second point is very different than traditional PR and Communications efforts, which typically measure their success according to audience awareness or opinion. To be clear, the metrics of success for PR and Communications have changed.

As a result, most professional communicators must adapt. For example, PR and Communications can no longer own the channels of external communications because there simply are too many. Just imagine trying to preapprove every message from any employee who mentions your brand. It simply is untenable. Further, PR and Communications teams can no longer own all relationships with external influencers or media. In many cases, subject matter experts outside of PR and Communications must be empowered and trusted to create and develop important relationships.

For an example, see our story of Joe Hughes of Accenture and Paul Greenberg in Chapter 3, Influence: It's Complicated.

To understand how this new model of communications can work, look at any large sales force. No VP of Sales owns every relationship with every customer. And no VP of Sales approves every customer presentation or every message that the sales people deliver to a customer. Instead, sales leaders provide tools, training, content, and ongoing coaching to empower their people for independent success. And then those leaders measure the performance of their people, they conduct periodic quality checks, and they talk to their people to get feedback on how they can make the entire team more effective.

The new model of PR and Communications requires more coordination and empowerment, and less command and control. It is, without doubt, a very uncomfortable change for many professional communicators; but tremendous impact will be made by those who find their way.

---

1. "Building Belief: A New Model for Activating Corporate Character and Authentic Advocacy." Arthur W. Page Society, March 2012. http://bit.ly/ArthurPage.

Product Marketers

Product marketers work within and possess unique insights into specific product lines or business units. They have a deep understanding of customer needs and brand value propositions. They understand the competition. They play a critical role in developing and executing market-facing strategies.

In a social employee program, they work with the extended product team, Market Intelligence and Research, and other internal teams to create strategies and plans. In addition, they collaborate with and advise the program team (mainly the social strategist) to help align employees and thought leaders against the external market for social outreach and engagement.

Legal

You will need to include legal expertise from inside your company for a number of purposes. First, this program will define and sometimes change the responsibilities and rewards of jobs within your organization. Your Human Resources team will need to be involved for those kinds of changes, and so will your Legal team.

Second, as you empower employees to engage in social media, you must ensure that your efforts comply with relevant laws in all of the jurisdictions where your employees operate. Further, you must include compliance guidance in your policies, training, and processes. Your Legal team will need to help you through all of that.

Human Resources

In most organizations, the HR or Personnel team governs guidelines for employees. You will need to change some of your policies in this program. HR also determines the structure of rewards, recognition, and retention strategies and programs, which need to support the goals of your social employee program. In addition, HR typically helps to recruit talent both internal and external to the company. Finally, as you define the roles and responsibilities of people who participate in the program, HR will need to help you ensure that you comply with relevant laws and internal guidelines.

Program Accounting or Finance

The Accounting and Finance teams manage your organization's money. They will help you to plan your budget and manage reporting as you spend it. As your program grows and your budget numbers grow, you will need to work with your Finance team to define your business case and to track progress against the business case. You will need them available to help you track funding and return on investment as the program progresses.

Finance will help you to determine how the program can be funded, how long you will get funded, and how much you can get funded. They can be your biggest ally in timing and messaging when requesting funding. You may also need help determining how some of your spending is treated within the company's accounting systems, especially if you develop any new software within the program.[2]

External Influencers

External market influencers are not employees of your organization, but they have strong online influence and expertise in a topic that is relevant to your organization's goals. These people maintain active social networks and a well-established reputation as authoritative, authentic, independent voices in the communities that you will target. Your employees who participate in the program will work to gain trust, build influence, and maintain collaborative relationships with targeted external influencers. Your participants will also encourage these external influencers to act as advocates for your organization and to share relevant branded information, opinions, and advice with their audience.

Information Technology

The program leadership is probably going to need to launch collaboration platforms of some type. IT will have an impact on or make decisions about which tools you can use, and your investment plan needs to sync with their

---

2. Most companies "capitalize" software development expenditures under certain conditions. Account treatments are beyond the scope of this book. Please consult your Finance team if you plan to invest in internal software development within your project.

investment plan. You need them to buy enabling technology and infrastructure at the right times in order to keep your program on track. It also helps ensure that all of your tools are safe and secure.

Agencies and Consultancies

When working with agency or consulting partners, it is important to candidly assess their strengths and weaknesses before you commit to their involvement. However, that is typically difficult to do in a proposal process. In fact, it takes time to discover their true strengths and weaknesses.

Many agencies and consultancies are still maturing their capabilities in social media, and, at the same time, social media are rapidly growing in complexity. Programs such as this involve technology change, process change, and work force transformation in the most sophisticated cases. Therefore, it is important to clearly understand your business goals, your requirements, and how each of your agency or consulting partners can help you.

In addition, take the time to clarify the terminology that you use within your program. Sometimes challenges arise from different definitions between the agency and the brand. In one case, we saw an agency defining *earned media* as online word-of-mouth that resulted from media buying, whereas the brand defined the term simply as word-of-mouth outcomes that resulted from social media efforts—not driven by paid media.

In this case, the agency defined *earned media* according to the world that creates value for the agency: media buying and planning. And that is a natural expectation, but it causes metrics to be calculated differently. For this brand, metrics that came from the agency were calculated in a different way than metrics that came from other sources, and it created significant issues when trying to determine whether one campaign or channel performed better or worse than others, or over time. It made spend optimization across campaigns very difficult, and it made feedback to the social employees difficult. In general, you should take the time to ensure that each metric and its calculations are the same among all team players.

Time Commitments

Teams always ask us how much time each person on the team should commit to the program. First, assignment to the team is a real commitment, especially for the program team (the people who will operationalize the changes) and program participants (the subject matter experts whom you are enabling). The program team will infuse the changes into their daily work, permanently. Instead of focusing on how long they will be engaged in the program, focus on the amount of support you will provide them and the plan for transitioning that support activity from the program to permanent support functions.

If your program is successful, the program team gradually works itself out of a job as the program participants incorporate your changes into their regular work and as the capabilities that you implement are adopted by more of the organization.

Your Next Steps

1. Evaluate current resources that could support program development and oversight.
2. Determine the most critical gaps in your available resources.
3. Determine steering committee participants and secure executive support for the steering committee.
4. Determine actions required to secure sponsorship and investment from the steering committee.

9

Manage the Journey

"To change something, never fight existing reality. Build a new model that makes the existing model obsolete."

— R. Buckminster Fuller

People with a vision inside of a company often feel trapped by existing processes or politics; or they feel that they do not have the ability to impact the decisions and budgets required to transform the organization. To help, this chapter provides a framework for managing change in large organizations and tips for leading the change you wish to see. Then, we address the changes that must occur with you, the change leader.

Culture and Change Management Will Make or Break Your Program

As more companies empower their employees in social media, some will execute the transition well, and some will not. Like all business concepts that change how business is done, execution makes the difference.

Some organizations will view social media enablement as an easy panacea that the CEO can simply delegate. Some will hire consultants with the right experience and expertise, and some will assume that the job is effectively done when they hire a social media strategist.

Many who execute poorly will blame the idea itself, and industry researchers will report the percentage of such programs that fail. The percentage will be greater than 50 percent, as with most transformational programs in the past.

Enabling a social work force requires difficult and significant choices. Simply deploying a few tools and giving everyone permission may make everyone feel better, but such approaches are quickly overrun when competitors invest more thoughtfully and more deeply into the socialization of their business operations.

As stated by Jason Breed of Accenture, "A social business isn't something that you switch on. It is a fundamental change in the way your people and your systems operate, every day."[1]

Most readers understand that social media is transforming business, but they may not always understand how to manage the journey. Sometimes, the change is happening to us, and we aren't sure how to best react or how to help ensure that the program achieves outcomes that we believe will benefit the organization.

In general, organizations that empower their employees in social media must wrestle with the following types of challenges:

1. **Internal Leadership:** People who know how to lead business transformation *and* understand how to use social media for business *and* have the support of senior leadership
2. **Functional Talent:** People with the specialized skills, knowledge, and internal relationships required to enable a specific business process or a specific business function

---

1. Breed, Jason. Personal interview. December 2012.

3. **Technical Talent:** People with the technical skills to create scalable technologies inside their organization and the wisdom to know when to bring in technologies from the outside
4. **Technology:** Infrastructure, applications, data, and flexibility to change as technologies evolve at a more rapid pace each year
5. **Organization:** The ways that responsibilities and resources are divided and combined
6. **Culture:** The foundational shared beliefs that people in a company value and aspire to realize; often dependent on the industry where the brand competes, including regulatory and other external factors

The Unique Role of Culture

In 2012, IBM demonstrated that the keys to accelerating widespread adoption of social media in business lie in two areas: (1) an organization's ability to build social business expertise among employees, and (2) encouraging behavioral changes that influence a wider cultural shift. So, culture is one of the most critical factors in making an organization more social; however, of all the challenges above, culture is typically the least understood and poorly addressed in large change programs.

In fact, respondents from only one-quarter of companies believe they are fully prepared to address the cultural changes that are associated with social business transformation.[2] Further, according to McKinsey & Company, half of all respondents believe that their companies' organizational structure is the biggest obstacle to achieving their digital priorities in general.[3] See Figure 9.1.

Understanding and Managing Culture

In many organizations, the ability to understand culture often impedes change within the culture.

One reason is that many people struggle to define culture in a way that allows them to address it in their change efforts. When asked to define culture, most people struggle.

---

2 Cortada, Jim, Eric Lesser, and Peter Korsten. "The Business of Social Business: What Words and How It's Done." IBM Institute for Business Value, 2012. http://bit.ly/IBM-Social-Business.
3 McKinsey & Company. "Minding Your Digital Business: McKinsey Global Survey Results." May 2012.

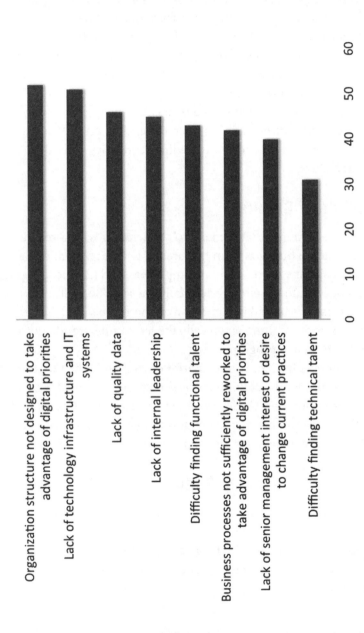

Figure 9.1 *Most significant challenges faced in meeting digital priorities. Percent of respondents.*

Source: Data from McKinsey & Company. "Minding Your Digital Business: McKinsey Global Survey Results." May 2012. http://bit.ly/DigitalHurdles.

The notion of culture has only been around for a couple of hundred years. Relative to most social sciences, it is very young. That may partially explain why culture is so poorly understood.

We like to think of culture as:

1. **Standards:** The standards to which employees are held.
2. **Beliefs:** The belief system of the company. Some companies believe that only professional communicators should be allowed to speak on behalf of the brand. Social brands know otherwise.
3. **Values:** The values of the people in the organization. Some brands place high value on employees who maintain a credible professional presence in social media. Some brands mistakenly undervalue that kind of employee presence and online influence.
4. **Understanding:** The mutual agreements and explanations carried by people in the organization, whether they realize them or not.

Those standards, beliefs, values, and understanding cause people to take decisions and behave in ways that become consistent throughout the organization.

So, if you want people to make decisions differently or to behave differently, then you must change the standards, beliefs, values, and understanding that people carry. How do you do that? You do it by changing the following controllable factors in the company:

1. **Processes:** If you want to empower thousands of people to publish in social media, you probably need to think about how you will create and distribute content to those people. How will you measure their performance throughout the process? The list of potential process changes is quite long.
2. **Policies:** Empowering employees in social media nearly always requires a brand to change its policies regarding the extent to which employees are permitted to publish about the company in social media.
3. **Systems:** The tool and technologies required to empower, support, measure, and optimize employee engagement are very different than the tools used by professional Communications or Marketing teams.

Align culture drivers with the business strategy, through:
- Processes
- Policies
- Systems
- Rewards
- Structure
- Leadership

New ways of acting permeate the company, via:
- How people make decisions
- How people act

Standards, beliefs, values, and understanding align with new behaviors.

Figure 9.2 *Steps in creating cultural change*

4. **Rewards:** For the most part, people are very busy. And they will focus their energy on whichever activities you reward. If you want them to begin a new activity, such as engaging in social media, you will need to think about how you will reward those who adopt the behaviors that you want them to adopt.
5. **Structure:** Organization often gets in the way. You may need to change the ways that teams are organized.
6. **Leadership:** Your executives must lead from the front. Set the example. If you want your people to change, you must do it first.

Figure 9.2 shows the order in which cultural changes can be managed.

Learning from the Past

There are lessons to be learned from past evolutions. Large change programs have been around for decades. Think about Y2K, CRM, supply chain transformation, or eBusiness—and the list goes on.

In 2002, Prosci asked 327 project leaders, consultants, and managers, "If you had the chance to do it again, what would you do differently?" The most common response was: "Utilize an effective and planned change management program."[4]

---

4. Prosci. *Business Process Reengineering Benchmarking Report.* Loveland, CO: Prosci Learning Center Publications, 2002.

In fact, the authors of that 2002 study found that the surveyed program leaders did not list technology, design, or strategy as their biggest challenges. Instead, they emphasized hurdles such as the following:

- Managers who were unwilling to assign necessary resources
- Employees who lost interest, impacting productivity and customers
- Valued employees who left the organization
- Unforeseen obstacles to the program that seemingly appeared from nowhere
- Lack of funding for the change
- Believing that change management was someone else's job
- Ignoring the people side of change until major resistance stalled a project or caused the project to fail

Leaders who empowered employees in social media told us that they often encounter similar types of challenges, such as:

- Inadequate funding for the design or implementation phases of the work
- Managers unwilling to support their employees' involvement in social media
- Demands that social media effort achieve greater accountability than other, existing channels
- People who feel like they understand how to use social media for business simply because they use it in their personal life
- Continually changing technologies, tools, skills, and best practices
- Fear of change or losing control
- Risks that people perceive and the extent to which the culture supports taking such risks

Danna Vetter of ARAMARK observed that one critical challenge was ". . . not as much skill gaps as continuing knowledge. Social networks adapt, evolve, and change every single day."[5]

---

5 Vetter, Danna. Personal interview. November 2012.

Neglecting the people side of change usually degrades program success and injects unnecessary risk into programs.

As Jeffrey Hiatt and Timothy Creasey state in their book *Change Management:*[6]

> Change management can not only mitigate these business risks, but in many cases avoid them entirely. Business leaders have the potential to not only manage resistance once it appears, but to prevent it in the first place.

Change Management Is New to Many Leaders

While culture and change management can make or break any program that depends upon people working differently than the past, internal change management is often new to Communications, Marketing, or IT professionals who now find themselves at the forefront of social business initiatives.

In addition, major technology shifts occur every ten years. The last major wave of transformation in business occurred during the 1990s, through the emergence of the internet, Y2K (i.e., year 2000), and business process reengineering initiatives. The people who led those programs in the late 1990s gained valuable experience in managing transformational change programs. But most of those program leaders have been promoted to senior roles since the late '90s, and they are no longer in a position to directly lead social business change management initiatives. Further, many of those former change leaders are unfamiliar with social media, or they work in departments that may not be at the forefront of social business initiatives. As a result, they are often not in a position to leverage their experience directly into social business transformation.

An Approach for Managing the Journey

When you begin to organize the change management portion of your program, consider the elements listed in Figure 9.3 and described in the following section.

An expanded and more detailed version of the figure is available for download on SocialMediaGovernance.com and SusanEmerick.com.

---

6 Hiatt, Jeffrey, and Timothy Creasey. *Change Management: The People Side of Change.* Loveland, CO: Prosci Research, 2003.

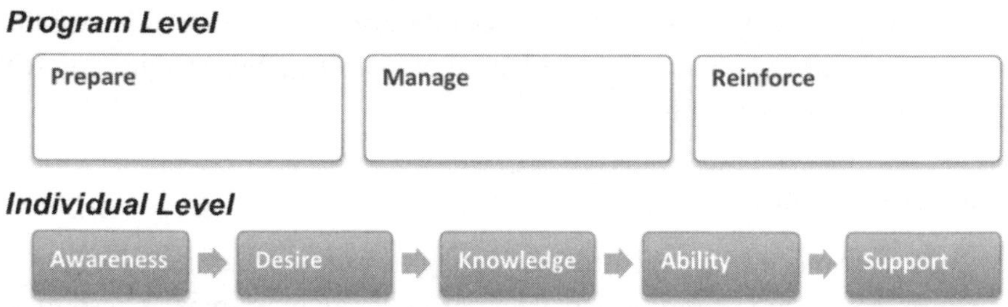

Program Level

Prepare	Manage	Reinforce

Individual Level

Awareness ▶ Desire ▶ Knowledge ▶ Ability ▶ Support

Figure 9.3 *Two levels of change management effort*

Program Level

At the program level, you will set the direction of the overall change effort by defining a clear purpose that your people will embrace, establishing plans and road maps, and ensuring that broad mechanisms are in place to reinforce the behavior changes required to achieve your program goals.

Prepare

Every successful change effort begins with a purpose. As stated by Anthony J. Bradley and Mark P. McDonald in their blog post on *Harvard Business Review*'s HBR Blog Network:

> Purpose is the reason people participate and contribute their ideas, experience and knowledge. They participate personally in social media because they value and identify with the purpose. They do so because they want to, rather than being told to as part of their job.[7]

Social media best create business value when a brand energizes people to take actions or propagate messages that advance the goals of the business, without having to pay traditional media rates for the effort.

And the only way to motivate people to carry forth your message or take actions and convince others to take actions on your behalf is to focus the brand's social media efforts on a *purpose* that resonates deeply within the audience, creating a shared belief they not only understand but feel compelled to share with their network.

---

7. Bradley, Anthony J., and Mark P. McDonald. "Social Media versus Knowledge Management." HBR Blog Network, *Harvard Business Review.* 26 October 2011.

The purpose that you define will depend upon the brand and its mission because it seeks to create a shared belief that people gather around and feel good about, like a campfire.

IBM Smarter Planet

At IBM, the Smarter Planet initiative highlights forward-thinking leaders in business, government, and society who demonstrate how smarter systems can achieve economic growth, near-term efficiency, sustainable development, and societal progress. The purpose of building a smarter planet deeply engages and motivates employees, customers, and other stakeholders in a multiyear effort that reaches around the world to inspire and educate us all about the power of technology in our lives. In addition, it creates stories that people want to experience and share, and it helps to guide the actions of employees as they engage in social media on behalf of the IBM brand. For example, see the post on IBM's A Smarter Planet Blog, wherein Mark Dean, IBM Fellow and Chief Technology Officer for IBM in the Middle East and Africa, describes IBM as the vanguard of the post-PC era from his personal vantage point as one of a dozen IBM engineers who designed the first machine.[8]

TOMS Shoes One for One

The founder of TOMS Shoes,[9] Blake Mycoskie, established his business on the principle of giving. Through the One for One initiative, with every pair of shoes purchased, TOMS gives a pair of shoes to a child in need. TOMS Giving Trips promote their purpose when the TOMS team travels to global destinations to deliver their contributions. On a recent trek to Central and South America, the team sought to help restore vision to patients at an eye clinic outside of Guatemala City, followed by an excursion to give shoes to Peruvian kids in two remote villages. Blake shares his treks by video blogging his trips to remote villages that benefit from his team's mission.

From shoes for children to high technology, every brand has a purpose that it can translate into something more social: something more shareable. The most successful social brands articulate a clear and compelling purpose

---

8. Dean, Mark. "IBM Leads the Way in the Post-PC Era." *A Smarter Planet Blog*. IBM, 10 August 2011. http://ibm.co/18cPGZA.

9 TOMS Shoes. http://www.toms.com/giving.

that is social in the eyes of their employees, their customers, and other stakeholders.

With a broad, compelling purpose defined, you should then answer the following questions:

- What is the scope of change?
  - How many people are affected?
  - Which business units?
  - Which business functions?
  - Which regions where the organization operates?
  - Which customer segments and channels?
  - Over what time frame?
- How much are we asking people to change?
  - How much additional change is happening outside the scope of our program?
  - How much resistance should we expect?
- Who will be the program sponsors?
  - How will we equip them for success?

With those questions answered, you can then assess and begin to equip your program sponsors.

Manage

Once you have program sponsors on board (explained in Chapter 8, Build Your Team), you can launch the change management effort, which will include creation and implementation of the following:

- Communication plans
- Coaching plans
- Training and education plans
- Sponsorship road maps
- Resistance-management plan

When developing the plans above, think about the culture of your organization. What makes people adopt new processes, new behaviors, and new beliefs? In most organizations, brute force is not the answer.

Consider this story from history: In the 1700s, Frederick the Great of Prussia was very keen for Germans to eat potatoes because he realized that, if they had two sources of carbohydrates (wheat and potatoes), there would be (1) less price volatility in bread and (2) lower risk of famine with two different crops to rely upon.

At the time, Germans felt that the potato looked unattractive, and 18th century Prussians ate very few vegetables. So, he first tried making it compulsory. There are even records of people being executed for refusing to grow potatoes.

That approach did not work, so he tried a different approach. He declared the potato a royal vegetable and stated that only the royal family could eat it. He planted it in a royal potato patch with guards who were instructed to guard over it night and day, but with secret instructions not to guard it very well.

As Rory Sutherland said, 18th-century peasants know there is one safe route in life: if something is worth guarding, it's worth stealing. Before long, there was a massive underground potato-growing operation in Germany. Frederick had rebranded the potato. In doing so, he realized the change he sought to drive: potato consumption among his people.[10]

As another example, it has been found that traffic signs flashing your speed and a smiling or frowning face prevent twice as many accidents compared to conventional speed cameras with penalties for speeding drivers. And the smiling signs cost 10 percent of the cost of the conventional cameras and penalties. In the case of speeding drivers, a small smiley face has a better chance of affecting behavior, and at lower cost.

Rory goes on to say, "There seems to be strange disproportionality at work in human problem solving, which is the tendency of the institution to deploy as much force as possible, and as much compulsion as possible; whereas the tendency of any person is to be influenced in reverse proportion to the amount of force applied."

Our sense of self-aggrandizement makes us believe that big, important problems need to have big, important—and expensive—solutions attached to them. But behavioral economics show that what changes our behaviors and our attitudes are not actually proportionate to the degree of expense entailed nor to the degree of force applied.

---

10. "Rory Sutherland. Life Lessons from an Ad Man." TED. July 2009. http://bit.ly/Rory-Sutherland. Video.

If you want more people to join your social media program, you must persuade them, rather than compel them. Make membership something to be coveted, not something to be fought. Begin by engaging early adopters with a strong professional reputation. Shine a light on their successes. Show how people in the program have fun and feel rewarded.

You might create a leader board that ranks the social media performance of the people in your program. Make it visible to all employees. Reward those who earn their way to the top, but do not punish the others. Design the leader board to inform and to motivate, not to demotivate or to punish.

Tell the stories of people who succeed. Publish the stories on your employee portal. Make the early adopters famous. Then, others will want to participate.

And make it tough to get accepted into the program. Slowly, more people will want to be in the program.

Reinforce

In order to ensure success, you must continually seek feedback from program sponsors and participants, then use that feedback to improve your work plan, your communications, and maybe even some of your change effort goals.

In general, you should assume that employees will hear and understand a small fraction of the messages that managers give them. Why? It is a simple fact of life that what we say and what people hear are not always the same thing. In addition, when people are busy and managing lots of priorities, managers often do not have the time to confirm that employees heard and understood the messages.

That is a big problem because people tend to translate the messaging to their personal situations. We all sometimes infer more than what is said, or we make assumptions when we do not hear clear answers to our questions.

Therefore, for every major audience group (e.g., executives, managers, and employees), you should create a framework that identifies gaps between the messages you deliver and the messages people carry in their minds. Then, think about how you will keep the project and the people on track throughout the duration of the program.

In addition, as you implement the planned changes, you and your organization will learn. You must accept that you cannot predict how things will evolve. In addition to the internal change that you are driving, factors outside of your organization and your control will almost definitely change or evolve. Competitors might change. Regulation might change. Customers might change. Therefore, you should prepare to evolve your effort and your policies to ensure that you continually protect employees and the company while maximizing the business value that your program creates.

Managing this kind of change requires commitment. It will not happen overnight. If you have started the journey and your program is not progressing as you hoped, take a step back and examine the structure of your program. Then, take a look at yourself and the people who are leading the initiative. As stated by S. Anthony Iannarino, who helps sales organizations to improve their performance, "[S]ometimes what needs to change is the effort you put into dragging your initiative all the way across the line."[11]

Individual Level

When you want to help individual employees or leaders support, enable, or achieve the change you seek to create, the following steps can help you to understand how much change is needed for each person and then plan specific types of support that you will provide.

Awareness

List the reasons that the change is needed. Specify how the change will help the organization and the individual. Review that list with the person, and rate the degree to which the person is aware of each reason.

Desire

List the factors and consequences for this person to create the desired change. Include benefits and consequences. Understand the degree to which

---

11. Iannarino, S. Anthony. "An Open Letter to Executive Management on Next Year's Change." *The Sales Blog.* 20 December 2012. http://bit.ly/ChangeEffort.

each factor motivates the person to act. Seek to understand why they would want to act and why they would want to avoid action.

Knowledge

List the skills and knowledge that the person will need to support or achieve the change. Assess the extent to which the person understands what the change must look like when completed. For complex changes, with multiple stages of evolution, also seek to understand whether they understand how interim stages should look.

Ability

Evaluate whether the person is capable of performing the change. Understand whether any behaviors might prevent the change. And understand which behaviors will support the change.

Support

Given all the preceding information, define the types of support that the person will need through the duration of the program. Examples include training, coaching, peer support, communication collaterals, incentives, and so on.

At IBM, Susan Emerick and her team established the Digital IBMer series, which showcased people who achieved business outcomes from social networking. They also published stories and information to help stimulate change and adoption, such as cyber security guidelines that help IBMers protect themselves and IBM while using social media.

That series continues to support internal change by combining inspiring success stories with training and support content that builds knowledge and skills across the IBM workforce.

Be the Change You Wish to See

If you want to control change, you must move ahead of it, not with it.

The journey begins with you. Your skills. Your relationships. Your personality.

Business transformation is a real skill set, including:

- Business case development
- Ability to lead and to make data-driven decisions
- Listening and empathy
- Work planning and program management
- Solution architecture
- Storytelling

Achieving significant competence requires years of experience. Therefore, give yourself some patience. If you feel like you aren't as good at it as you might like to be, there are people around the world who can help you. Seek them out.

As observed by Danna Vetter, VP of Consumer Marketing Strategy at ARAMARK, the efforts described in this book are, ". . . not a project you can fly solo on. You have to be someone that is inclusive of others around the organization and who can be flexible to ideas and methods others might bring to the table. You need others around the table."[5]

Also, you will find additional helpful resources, lessons, and tools on the authors' Web sites: SocialMediaGovernance.com and SusanEmerick.com.

Your Next Steps

1. Identify the attributes of your organization's culture that will affect your social employee program.
2. Candidly assess your personal strengths in the skills required to lead change, and recruit people who are strong in the areas where you are not.
3. Identify people who successfully led large change programs in your organization. Ask them what they learned along the way.
4. Evaluate management readiness to support a social employee program, and map out actions to drive adoption.
5. Think about how you will identify and find the early adopters in your organization.

10

The Future of the Social Work Force

"The difference between what we do and what we are capable of doing would suffice to solve most of the world's problem."

— Mahatma Gandhi

This chapter examines emerging or slowly evolving trends that will affect social employee programs five to ten years in the future. Nothing in this chapter will come to full fruition in the next year or two. And we strived to describe somewhat esoteric concepts in straightforward terms, so that you can incorporate them into your thinking on how to prepare your organization for the future.

People Will Change

In the next five to ten years, change will continue to be the norm. Even more so. Technology changes will continue to accelerate, global marketplaces will continue to integrate, and new opportunities will continue to reveal themselves. Through it all, the foundation of social media will remain: people. And we, the people, will need to wrestle with two important factors that will change the way we work and play. First, we will all be part of a world and a work force that is more social and more digital. Second, we will all find our personal and professional reputations becoming more exposed and accessible to people whom we may not even know. This section explains those changes and their implications.

Social Media Will Be Natural for Tomorrow's Leaders and Workers

Younger employees have a presence in social media before they take their first job. Some people call today's youth digital natives because they have never known a world that was not digital and, in more recent years, social. In fact, many had their social footprint established for them on the day they were born, when their parents posted pictures online to celebrate their birth. As they come of age, social media are a natural part of their daily lives. They are naturally accustomed to navigating across various social networks and platforms and are more likely to naturally bridge personal and professional participation in social media.

In addition, they have no desire to abandon their social media presence for the following reasons: First, they see their personal brand lasting longer than any individual job or career. Second, they tend to be more open to sharing their expertise as professionals. Third, they understand the inherent value of an online reputation (good or bad).

And, in the United States at least, the National Labor Relations Board already decided that brands can't stop them. Specifically, the NLRB has consistently decided that employees' rights to comment on workplace conditions or engage in concerted activity extend into their personal social media— meaning that employees can discuss working conditions with each other through social networks, in public view.

As today's youth become tomorrow's leaders, they will already understand social media more innately than most adults today. Whereas brands today create significant training and education to ensure that people understand social media, much of the training and adoption effort will be less intensive in 5 to 10 years.

Today, we have to educate and train employees to use social venues, and we often have to help them to understand the inherent value of building reputation and sharing expertise online. In five years, that training will be unnecessary.

However, we will still need to train people to use social media effectively for business. Greg Gerik, who is a global social media leader at 3M, said, "There is wide misunderstanding of social networks and programs. Many people make the assumption that, 'I know what this is because I do it in my personal life,' but their personal experience and knowledge doesn't translate to business."[1] The need for training in the context of business uses of social media will continue far into the future, especially as social media technologies and data grow more integrated with the technologies, data, and business processes inside of organizations.

Online Reputation Will Be Like Credit Scores: Everyone Will Have One, Whether They Like It or Not

"With every trade we make, comment we leave, person we flag, badge we earn, we leave a reputation trail." So said Rachel Botsman,[2] who writes and speaks globally on the power of collaboration and sharing through social technologies.

In the physical world, we often rely on people we know to tell us whether we can trust people who are new to us. As more of us engage in more social interactions, online reputation will also be the currency that tells people whom they can trust. But online reputation will be more accessible and more transparent than personal reputations passed by word of mouth today. In fact, the data that composes our reputations online will be so pervasive that the résumé will become a relic.

---

1. Gerik, Greg. Personal interview. November 2012.
2. "Rachel Botsman: The Currency of the New Economy Is Trust." TED. June 2012. http://www.ted.com/talks/rachel_botsman_the_currency_of_the_new_economy_is_trust.html. Video.

For example, consider Stack Overflow, which is a platform where experienced programmers can ask other programmers highly detailed technical questions. This site receives 5,500 questions per day, and 80 percent receive correct responses. Users gain reputation in many ways, but it all boils down to earning recognition from other users.

Soon after the site grew in popularity, users started putting their reputation scores on their résumés, and recruiters now search the site for programmers to hire. In response, Stack Overflow introduced reputation dashboards that provide a priceless window into how someone really behaves and what people think of them. The reputation that these programmers generate in one place has value far beyond that site, where the people with the real talent rise to the top.

Rachel Botsman also suggested that people should each own their reputation data. It should travel with us from one online community to another. If someone establishes reputation in one online community, they should be able to use that reputation when they join another community. In fact, online reputation could become the credit rating of the future, and startups like Connect.Me,[3] Legit,[4] and Trust Cloud[5] are working today to make that happen.

On the other hand, systems like these should ensure that they have measures in place to prevent abuse of the data they collect and distribute. As Constantin Basturea of Accenture said, "Reputation doesn't include only what we do right, but also things we do wrong. Should everything be counted in our reputation scores? There are people who argue that, for example, Google should 'forget' information about each one of us after certain time periods, because any other approach will affect negatively our capacity to develop as individuals."[6]

Technology Will Change

Within each of our lifetimes, technology has dramatically altered nearly every aspect of our lives. The pace of technological change will only increase in coming years as machines develop intelligence to rival people, as more and more tasks become automated, and as analytical tools and capabilities grow faster, cheaper, and more accessible. While many people will feel

---

3. https://connect.me/.
4. http://legit.co.
5. http://TrustCloud.com.
6. Kurzweil, Ray. Personal interview. February 2013.

challenged by these changes, we hope the following section helps you to see opportunity for innovation and evolution.

The Singularity: Machines as Smart as Humans

In an interview with McKinsey & Company, Ray Kurzweil explained that information technology is growing and evolving exponentially, but our intuition about the future is not exponential; it's linear. People think things will grow at the pace of 1, 2, 3, etc. And 30 steps later you're at 30. In reality, information technology grows exponentially. It grows more like 1, 2, 4, 8—and at step 30, you're at a billion.[7]

Because we tend to think in terms of linear growth, we tend to underestimate the impacts that future technologies will have on our lives and our organizations.[7]

Futurists like Ray Kurzweil predict that, by the year 2029, we will have hardware powerful enough to simulate the human brain. As a result, Kurzweil predicts that we will have human-level intelligence in a machine by 2029.

By 2045, according to Kurzweil, the portion of our civilization's intelligence that exists within computers and machines will expand 20-fold. Machines will be able to apply the same levels of intelligence as humans. This is often referred to as *the Singularity,* and most futurists agree that we simply cannot imagine how the Singularity will impact jobs, organizations, or society.[8]

Although we cannot fully imagine how things will change, we should understand that things will change more suddenly and dramatically than we expect. Because information technology grows its capabilities along an exponential scale, each year of progress brings significantly more change than the year before. As a result, the pace of change essentially increases each year. Our expectations must do the same.

Too often, when we plan for the future, we underestimate how much technology and our world will change. When we look back only three or four years, very few people used wikis, blogs, or social networks. Now, nearly everyone uses them for work, personal matters, or both. The pace of change will be only greater in coming years.

---

7. "IT Growth and Global Change: A Conversation with Ray Kurzweil." McKinsey & Company, 29 February 2012. http://bit.ly/Kurzweil-Interview. Video.
8. "Technological Singularity." *Wikipedia.* http://bit.ly/The-Singularity.

Increasing Automation

On one hand, every new advancement of technology increases the efficiency and the social glue of trust to make sharing easier and easier. On the other hand, as machines approach the ability to replicate human intelligence, more and more human interactions will be automated.

In their book entitled *Race Against the Machine*,[9] Erik Brynjolfsson and Andrew McAfee show how technology has automated jobs that originally required people interacting with other people. Examples include call centers that use computers to answer customer questions and toll booths that use computers to charge people for driving on a highway.

In his 1996 book entitled, *The End of Work*,[10] Jeremy Rifkin suggested that ". . . we are entering a new phase in world history—one in which fewer and fewer workers will be needed to produce the goods and services for the global population." In fact, Rifkin wrote that "more sophisticated software technologies are going to bring civilization ever closer to a near-workerless world."

In 1983, Nobel Prize winner Wassily Leontief stated, "[T]he role of humans as the most important factor of production is bound to diminish in the same way that the role of horses in agricultural production was first diminished and then eliminated by the introduction of tractors."[11]

As we approach increasing automation of the jobs performed by people, and as machine intelligence approaches that of our coworkers, we must wonder how online relationships might be affected. To what extent will interactions that occur between people today become automated and remove people from the equation? Like programmed stock traders today.

As organizations seek to industrialize social media and make it more scalable, at what point does automation take away the value of personal connections that occur through social media?

---

9. Brynjolfsson, Erik, and Andrew McAfee. *Race against the Machine: How the Digital Revolution is Accelerating Innovation, Driving Productivity, and Irreversibly Transforming Employment and the Economy.* Lexington, MA: Digital Frontier Press, 2011.
10. Rifkin, Jeremy. *The End of Work: The Decline of the Global Labor Force and the Dawn of the Post-Market Era.* New York: Jeremy P. Tarcher, 16 April 1996.
11. "The Long-Term Impact of Technology on Employment and Unemployment: A National Academy of Engineering Symposium." *National Perspective: The Definition of Problems and Opportunities.* Washington, DC: National Academy Press, 30 June 1983.

And how will these trends affect people who develop a strong personal presence in social media? Will those people become more valuable to brands, or will the value they create be gradually automated by ever faster, smarter, and more human-like computers?

We believe that automation is not necessarily good or bad. In reality, you should think about your social media operations as a set of processes, and the value of automation will vary for different steps. The same is true for outsourcing.

For example, some people have said that a brand, "should never outsource tweeting." But that level of opinion fails to recognize that there are a lot of steps in "tweeting" on behalf of a brand. Some of those steps can be automated, and some can be outsourced very effectively. Specifically, when a brand engages in social media, the full process typically involves the following steps:

1. Research the online conversations that affect your brand, and determine how you will engage, where, when, and with whom.
2. Select tools to monitor conversations; select tools to engage in conversations.
3. Configure tools.
4. Train your people.
5. Define how you will measure success. What will be your operating metrics?
6. Implement a measurement regimen (e.g., daily, weekly, monthly, quarterly).
7. Monitor online conversations.
8. Identify engagement opportunities.
9. Create content to publish.
10. Post the content into social media; respond to audiences as appropriate.

Some of the steps above can be automated. Some can be outsourced. The simple reality is that "tweeting" is not so simple inside of a brand.

As demand for social media skills increases, and as "digital natives" increase their share of the work force, the supply of people with social media skills will also increase. As supply increases, prices naturally fall. So, on average, the value of any person with a given presence in social media will decrease over time.

In addition, technological progress will ensure that fewer and fewer people are required to achieve the same level of output and outcomes over time. As more people possess the skills necessary to engage in social media, supply will increase, and as companies can achieve more output with fewer people, demand for people will decrease. Those two factors will conspire to drive down the value of the average social media practitioner and, eventually, social media skills will become a basic requirement for most workers, just like e-mail and word-processing skills today.

However, we believe that there will always be demand for people with exceptional skills, exceptional expertise in technologies that enable them to achieve greater outcomes than their peers, and unique domain knowledge sought by customers and business partners. Ultimately, social media engagement skills will become as commonly required as a college degree, and the most important determinant of employee value will be similar to those of today: education, relationships, and knowledge built through experience that is unique and valued by employers.

More Powerful and Accessible Analytics

Few people dictate a memo or hand-write a document and send it to a typist. People are expected to write their own documents because word-processing technologies are so pervasive.

Similarly, in the future, people will be expected to answer more analytical questions. For example, imagine looking at your mobile phone and quickly understanding:

1. The best times of day to engage with your target audiences
2. The attributes of your content that make your content perform the best
3. The people online who can help you to achieve your performance goals
4. The content produced by your peers that you should amplify to achieve team goals
5. Changes you can make to your content to increase the likelihood that it will be amplified by your peers
6. How you are performing relative to peers, and the best practices for improving your performance

Three trends are conspiring to make it easier for people to perform their own analytics rather than relying on highly trained specialists.

1. **Easier-to-integrate data sources:** Cloud computing, application programming interfaces (APIs), and advancements in user interfaces are making it easier for people to access more data from more sources than ever before.

2. **Easier-to-use advanced analytics:** As computers grow exponentially more powerful, it becomes cheaper and easier to place sophisticated analytical tools into the hands of the average person. For example, think about the levels of analysis that anyone can perform at zero cost within Google Analytics. As of this writing, you can see how users travel through your Web site, in real time. You can see how the traffic varies by source country, or which Web sites that refer them to your Web site, and you can do it all with a few clicks of a mouse. In the world of advanced analytics, tools like Tableau Software make it easy to pull data from multiple sources and display it in easy-to-understand and easy-to-manipulate charts.

3. **Increasing familiarity with social media and how it creates value for individuals and organizations:** As more people use social media for business, more people will understand how social media creates business value—how it can decrease operating costs or increase revenues. As more people experience these benefits from social media, their understanding of the relationships between social media and business value will become more intuitive.

As these three trends converge, analytical tools become easier to use and less expensive to acquire. Over time, more people will be expected to understand and use them as part of their daily work. Just like most people today are expected to understand word processing and spreadsheets for many jobs.

Organizations Will Change

In the year 2013, companies are finally figuring out how to embed social capabilities into business processes throughout their organizations. Social media are no longer confined to Marketing and PR. In fact, organizations are now using social media, social capabilities, and the data that fuel them in most every functional area. Examples include the following:

- Using social media data to:
  - Understand customers
  - Identify ideas for improving products and services or creating new products or services
  - Designing and targeting communications across digital and traditional channels
  - Following market and competitive trends

- Empowering greater collaboration across traditional boundaries, such as:
  - Letting customers and employees work together to resolve product issues
  - Letting channel partners and employees collaborate more deeply during sales processes
  - Letting recruiters and employees work together to attract, identify, and screen better job candidates more efficiently
  - Using social media as a channel to communicate with customers for marketing, selling, and branding

All of the uses listed above are why companies like IBM predict that, by 2022, social technology will enable four out of every five customer transactions.[12] That does not mean that four of every five transactions will occur within social networks; it means that social media will play a role in 80 percent of customer transactions.

Based upon the road maps we help our clients to define, we believe that most companies will achieve that level of social business before 2022—probably within the next five years. In many cases, we are seeing clients plan for that level of social media integration within three to five years.

This will occur because businesses will slowly embed social capabilities into their business processes because making processes social will increase the value yielded to the brand. One by one, processes will transform.

---

12. "Liking Isn't Leading." IBM, 2010. Available at http://bit.ly/like-lead

Therefore, one by one, departments, business units, and entire brands will also transform. The changes will happen slowly—between 2013 and 2022, for example. But they will happen.

And one day, we will all pause, look around, and slowly notice that our organizations have transformed. Just like one day, we all looked around, and e-mail was simply everywhere. It happened slowly. Most of us may not even remember when it happened. But today it is simply everywhere. So will be the path of social business transformation.

Results for Workers and Leaders

As technology changes, customers change, and our organizations change, then our employees and managers have no choice but to change. In general, workers will change how they work as customers grow more empowered and business processes grow more social. In order to succeed as leaders, we who manage people will also have to change for the better. Figure 10.1 summarizes the changes we see happening, as well as their effects on workers and leaders.

Workers Will Change How They Work

As customers grow more empowered and business processes grow more social, more employees will develop social media skills. Just like everyone knows how to e-mail, everyone will know how to use social media tools to get work done.

Along the way, employees will publish more—both inside and outside of their organizations—because publishing will be second nature. Through things like short tweets, occasional blog posts, collaboration platforms, and on-demand video conferencing, more employees will produce more content that establishes their reputation and authority in the workplace and beyond.

Today, anyone can publish their résumé via LinkedIn. And application extensions let anyone add a portfolio of presentations via SlideShare, creative designs via Behance, or thought leadership via blogs. Publishing will become more normal, and information will become more accessible. As a result, people inside and outside of organizations will collaborate more and more. The way work gets done will change, as it already has in the past 20 years. We will become even more global, more collaborative, and more efficient.

As a result, leaders will also need to change.

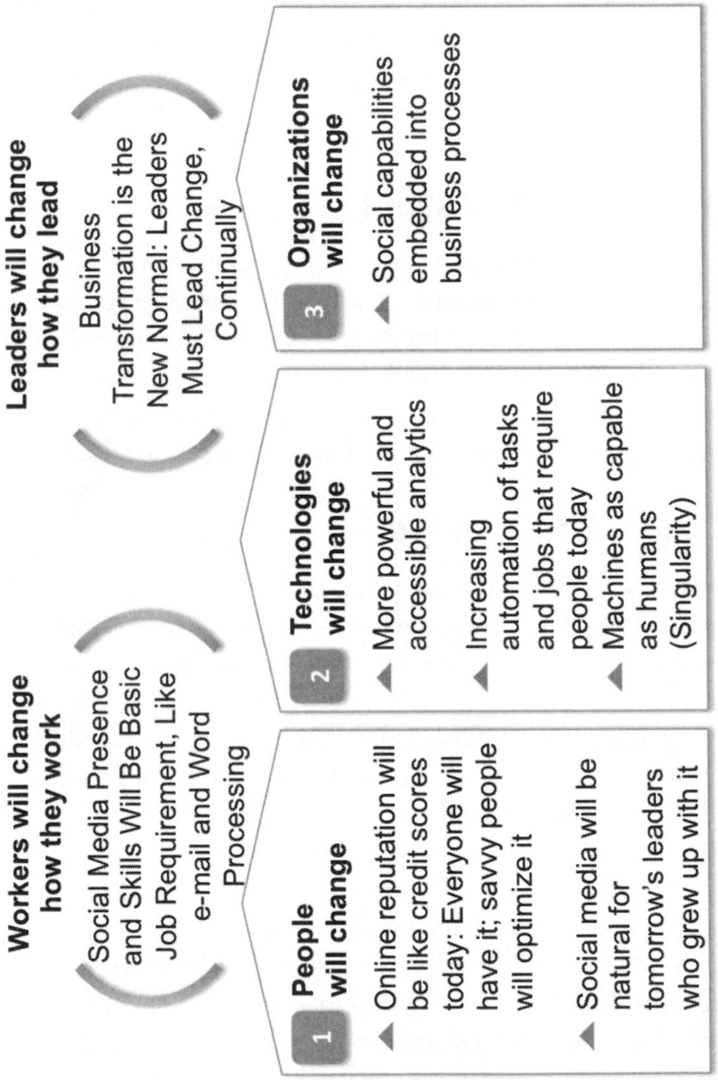

Workers will change how they work

Social Media Presence and Skills Will Be Basic Job Requirement, Like e-mail and Word Processing

Leaders will change how they lead

Business Transformation is the New Normal: Leaders Must Lead Change, Continually

1 People will change

◄ Online reputation will be like credit scores today: Everyone will have it; savvy people will optimize it

◄ Social media will be natural for tomorrow's leaders who grew up with it

2 Technologies will change

◄ More powerful and accessible analytics

◄ Increasing automation of tasks and jobs that require people today

◄ Machines as capable as humans (Singularity)

3 Organizations will change

◄ Social capabilities embedded into business processes

Figure 10.1 *Long-term trends affecting social employees and leaders*

Leaders Will Change How They Lead

For all the folks selling *social business,* who think that they will sway business leaders with the claim that "the world is changing and you must change with it," we offer the following quote from the 1993 book *Reengineering the Corporation:*[13]

> Advanced technologies, the disappearance of boundaries between national markets, and the altered expectations of customers who now have more choices than ever before have combined to make the goals, methods, and basic organizing principles of the classical corporation sadly obsolete. Renewing their competitive capabilities isn't an issue of getting the people in these companies to work harder, but of learning to work differently. This means that companies and their employees must unlearn many of the principles and techniques that brought them success for so long.

That was published 20 years ago.

Yes, social technologies are dramatically altering how we communicate as humans. And the impacts on our organizations over the next few years will be profound and exciting. And, due to the technological acceleration that we describe previously, the pace of change will only continue to increase.

But, the exceptional leaders of today and tomorrow understand that continual change is not just a sales pitch. It is reality. In fact, business transformation needs to be a way of life. Business transformation will continue for the next ten years in new forms that we do not imagine today—just like it did ten years ago, and just like it is doing now.

Therefore, the most important challenge lies not in the changes themselves, but in finding experienced people who can lead large business transformation programs *and* who truly understand how to operate social media at scale. These are the skills that will differentiate the leaders of social business over the next few years, and every organization needs to find and nurture people with business transformation skills.

---

13. Hammer, Michael, and James Champy. *Reengineering the Corporation: A Manifesto for Business Revolution.* New York, NY. HarperBusiness. 1993.

Winners Will Empower Their Employees in Social Media

According to Deloitte, return on assets for public companies in the United States shrank by 75 percent from 1965 to 2009.[14] The decline did not happen abruptly, but occurred through a slow and sustained erosion over decades. And the decline did not depend upon shorter-term economic cycles.

Throughout the decline, businesses largely responded by squeezing out costs wherever possible. They invested in enterprise applications designed to standardize and automate business processes, and they sent work activities to lower-cost locations around the world. Throughout the evolution, most organizations viewed employees as a simple cost that needed to be minimized.

But companies can only take out costs for so long. After a while, it gets harder and harder to take out any more costs. Even so, the pressure to increase returns has continued. And, while we do not claim to know the solution for all companies in all industries, we firmly believe that most organizations now have an opportunity to invest in employees as assets who deliver increasing value to the marketplace.

Given the appropriate tools and skill development, there will be tremendous opportunities for smart brands to invest thoughtfully and strategically in their employees with significant returns on their investments.

But innovation is hard because it means challenging what we take for granted or things that we think are obvious. As Sir Ken Robinson said, "The great problem for transformation is the tyranny of common sense."[15] People often think that things cannot be done any other way because "that's the way it's done."

In December 1862, when facing a civil war between the two halves of the nation he so loved, U.S. President Abraham Lincoln stated, "The dogmas of the quiet past are inadequate to the stormy present. The occasion is piled high with difficulty and we must rise with the occasion. As our case is new,

14. Hagel III, John, John Seely Brown, and Lang Davison. "Measuring the Forces of Long-Term Change: The 2009 Shift Index." Deloitte Center for the Edge, 2009.
15. "Ken Robinson: Bring on the Learning Revolution!" TED. February 2010. http://bit.ly/LearningRev. Video.

so we must think anew, and act anew. We must disenthrall ourselves, and then we will save our country."[16]

Many of the ideas that enthrall us were formed to suit the needs of the past. But the world is changing. Technology is changing. People are changing. And the organizations that thrive are those that recognize and embrace change as necessary for their future—right now.

Even so, changing requires that we examine the fundamental assumptions about the world that we take for granted, then change those assumptions to the degree that they no longer fit our world.

It is hard to recognize what we take for granted. The reason is that we take it for granted. For example, most people over 25 years of age wear a wristwatch. But today's teenagers do not wear them. They've been raised in a world that is digitized and the time is everywhere, so they have no need for a wristwatch.

As Alfred Chandler noted in *The Visible Hand*,[17] it was not until the railroad and electronic communication systems took hold that a new class of worker emerged: the modern manager. And, while we may feel like the Web has been around for our entire lives, the Web is less than 20 years old. To be fair, the infrastructure supporting the post-digital revolution—where technology is at the service of people—is still under construction.

Ultimately, technology gives people power. And they can leverage it for the benefit of themselves, or for their organizations. As more people grow more empowered through social media, many brands will need to rethink their approach to intellectual property and the degree to which they should wholly own the channels they use to communicate with external audiences. Further, we can only imagine how the jobs of managers will continue to change as technology accelerates, as employees grow more empowered, and as brands that invest in their people grow to become the most powerful brands on Earth.

---

16. Lincoln, Abraham. "Annual Address to Congress—Closing Remarks." Washington, DC: 1 December 1862. Taken from Basler, Roy P, ed. *The Collected Works of Abraham Lincoln*. The Abraham Lincoln Association, 1953. http://bit.ly/Lincoln-Quote.

17. Chandler, Jr., Alfred DuPont. *The Visible Hand: The Managerial Revolution in American Business*. Cambridge, MA: Belknap Press, 1993.

Your Next Steps

1. Pause for a moment and think about whether you really under-stand how technological, demographic, and economic factors are affecting your business today. Do you really have a firm grasp on the data that describes what is happening?

2. Give yourself periodic opportunities to consider the potential threats and opportunities for your organization when the pace of change accelerates in coming years.

3. Identify the three to five most important technologies to your organization, and determine how their accelerating evolution could affect your business and your competitors.

4. Imagine a world in which the answers to every analytical ques-tion await you in a device that you carry in your pocket.

5. Consider the extent to which creativity and synthesis could become more important in your organization, and think about how you will source those skills in the future—or how you will nurture them in yourself.

INDEX

O

P

R

informIT.com THE TRUSTED TECHNOLOGY LEARNING SOURCE

PEARSON **InformIT** is a brand of Pearson and the online presence
for the world's leading technology publishers. It's your source
for reliable and qualified content and knowledge, providing
access to the top brands, authors, and contributors from
the tech community.

✦Addison-Wesley   **Cisco Press**   EXAM/**CRAM**   **IBM** Press.   **QUe**   ✂ PRENTICE HALL   **S∧MS** | Safari

LearnIT at InformIT

Looking for a book, eBook, or training video on a new technology? Seeking timely and relevant information and tutorials? Looking for expert opinions, advice, and tips? **InformIT has the solution.**

- Learn about new releases and special promotions by subscribing to a wide variety of newsletters. Visit **informit.com/newsletters**.

- Access FREE podcasts from experts at **informit.com/podcasts**.

- Read the latest author articles and sample chapters at **informit.com/articles**.

- Access thousands of books and videos in the Safari Books Online digital library at **safari.informit.com**.

- Get tips from expert blogs at **informit.com/blogs**.

Visit **informit.com/learn** to discover all the ways you can access the hottest technology content.

Are You Part of the **IT** Crowd?

Connect with Pearson authors and editors via RSS feeds, Facebook, Twitter, YouTube, and more! Visit **informit.com/socialconnect**.

FREE
Online Edition

Your purchase of *The Most Powerful Brand on Earth* includes access to a free online edition for 45 days through the **Safari Books Online** subscription service. Nearly every Prentice Hall book is available online through **Safari Books Online**, along with thousands of books and videos from publishers such as Addison-Wesley Professional, Cisco Press, Exam Cram, IBM Press, O'Reilly Media, Que, and Sams.

Safari Books Online is a digital library providing searchable, on-demand access to thousands of technology, digital media, and professional development books and videos from leading publishers. With one monthly or yearly subscription price, you get unlimited access to learning tools and information on topics including mobile app and software development, tips and tricks on using your favorite gadgets, networking, project management, graphic design, and much more.

Activate your FREE Online Edition at
informit.com/safarifree

STEP 1: Enter the coupon code: RRVHDDB.

STEP 2: New Safari users, complete the brief registration form.
Safari subscribers, just log in.

If you have difficulty registering on Safari or accessing the online edition,
please e-mail customer-service@safaribooksonline.com